# Preface

Hitherto, a relatively large amount of partial and fragmentary literature concerning the principles of war has been found here and there, but a systematized work has not existed up to now.

There are difficulties in systematization of the principles of war that shed light on its true nature (theory that has the character of developing dialectically from rationality and actual proof). But in view of the state of knowledge of modern young officers, etc., as stated in the Forward, since it is fully realized that study of the principles of war is an urgent necessity, systematization was undertaken through the Board for Study of the Principles of War.

In this systematization, under the direction of Instructors Onizawa, Nozoe, and Yamanouchi, and with Instructors Daihachi Matsumoto, Kiyofuji, and Maeda as a nucleus, a draft was compiled in March 1967 and, by great effort, was generally completed in August, and its essentials were presented incrementally through the *Kanbu-gakkō-kiji* [*Staff College News*].

Fortunately, it received a favorable reception from all of you readers, and now, in response to your request that it be brought out in book form, it has been edited by Instructor Tomizawa and has reached the stage of publication as a reference work for beginning students of military tactics. Of course, this book is only one step in the study, and there is believed to be much room for improvement, but the book is being presented hurriedly for use by beginning students in diligently teaching themselves, and it is hoped that you readers will give us your suggestions and corrections.

Finally, profound gratitude is expressed to Nishiura, Chief of the Military History Department of the National Defense College, who provided guidance concerning the approach to the principles of war; to Tanaka Shoten [Tanaka Book Company], that devoted exceptional effort to the publication; and to Colonel Toshinobu Ikeda and to the Board members listed below.

January 1969

Kaoru Aoki, Maj Gen, Board Chairman
Sekiteru Yamada, Maj Gen, Board Vice Chairman

Board for Study of the Principles of War
Ground Self-Defense Force Staff College

Urban area

Swampy land

Lakes and marshes

Woodland terrain

Mountainous area

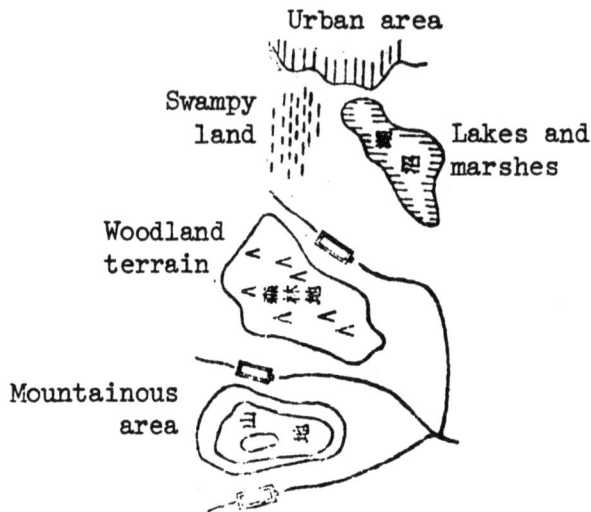

Members of the Board for Study of the Principles of War

| | | |
|---|---|---|
| Kentarō Anabuki | Nobuyuki Suzuki | Ryōichi Funakoshi |
| Minoru Ueki | Seiichi Tauchi | Hachirō Maeda |
| Kaoru Onisawa | Kenji Takagi | Shōsuke Maki |
| Yūkō Kashiwaba | Inao Tanaka | Masaya Maki |
| Makoto Katō | Sunao Chamura | Katsunori Makino |
| Toshio Kamo | Matsuji Tomisawa | Tomohiro Matsui |
| Kokki Kiyofuji | Mitsukuni Narishige | Daihachi Matsumoto |
| Yasushi Kunigo | Shōki Noguchi | Yonejirō Matsumoto |
| Osamu Kōno | Naoyuki Nozoe | Tomoyoshi Miki |
| Keijirō Sakae | Takatomo Hamaguchi | Takeji Yamauchi |
| Harutaka Sasaki | Hitoshi Fujiyoshi | Taneaki Yamanouchi |
| Hisashi Shibata | Kiyomi Haruyama | Kazuo Yamamura |

It is very gratifying here to be able to submit to the officers of the Ground Self-Defense Force the *Introduction to the Principles of War*, which has brought together the study results of our school's Board for Study of the Principles of War.

It goes without saying that explaining the "principles of combat" and the many other principles (except doctrine matters) presented in textbooks, as well as the various fundamentals which are omitted from the textbooks but are the basis for the various principles, is the point of departure for improvement in strategic capability.

However, in order to be able, under all situations, to make accurate decisions and to form creative plans that accomplish the mission, it is absolutely necessary ordinarily to identify these principles in all military histories and other books on military science, to give careful thought and consideration to them, to train in them through applied tactics and field exercises, and to incorporate them into one's own capability.

This book sought and analyzed proven lessons in military history concerning the principles of war considered particularly important up to about the end of World War II, compared and carefully examined well-known ancient and modern books on military science, and consolidated and systematized the material, and it is believed to be a good reference book for young officers seeking to study strategy and tactics. Of course, in the implementation of applied tactics, field exercises, etc., it should be borne in mind that the principles of war presented in this book should not be followed blindly in making one's decisions, but, as stated above, one must confront matters with something that, through diligent study, has become an integral part of one's own capability.

In regard to principles of war that must be added anew after World War II (such as, for example, the principle of war of countering indirect aggression), there must be continuing study and a quest for critiques everywhere, in order to ensure greater perfection.

January 1969

Haruo Umezawa, Lt Gen
Commandant, Ground Self-Defense Force Staff College

## Table of Contents

## Part I.  INTRODUCTION

### Chapter I.  Initial Remarks

In connection with the planning of the Yalu River river-crossing attack at the beginning of the Russo-Japanese War, General Tamemoto Kuroki, Commander of the [Japanese] First Army, in one paragraph of his instructions to his assembled staff, stated that, "In the military operations of the First Army, particularly the operations at the beginning of the war, if we do not act so that future historians cannot raise even one point of criticism, we should fail in our samurai duty.  ...  Since the plan was made with such care and logic, even if the worst should happen, that would not be a matter for regret; it would be divine will. ... and I ask that you perform so that future readers of history will judge that it was with complete dedication."

And France's famous military commander, Marshal Foch, said, "The art of war, like other arts, has its fundamental principles.  If that were not the case, war would not be an art.  War is learnable and is something that must be learned; it is an understanding of the true nature of war gained through extensive and intensive study of military history that is the basis for study of the art of war."  Again, in regard to the principles of war, he also said, "There is a gap between knowing and having ability, but with absolutely no knowledge, it is not possible to move in a single jump to having ability.  In contrast, if one has the knowledge, one can have the ability.  Knowledge is a necessary condition. If one has knowledge, in a short time one would gain confidence, and confidence brings accurate decisions."  These are wise statements presenting suggestions for both the East and the West concerning the principles of war and the development of capability with them; and, in general, for persons studying the art of war, they clarify the principles and rules of warfare (the so-called principles of war) and show the importance of knowing them and developing the ability to apply them.

Particularly for beginning students, it is believed that the essence of improving tactical capability is, first, studying these "principles of warfare" fundamentally and scientifically, then deepening one's understanding of the "knowledge," making this "knowledge" one's guide, accumulating "substantiating evidence" from "military history," developing this base for judgment (capability), and training and improving judgment (capability) through applied tactics (map and terrain exercises, war games, and field exercises).

This book has the objective, from the above viewpoint, of providing beginning students of tactics with deeper understanding of the principles of land warfare and with a basis for future improvement in tactical capability.

### Chapter II.  The Essence of Warfare and the Characteristics of Land Warfare

1.  The essence of warfare

    a.  What is warfare?

War is a clash of opposing wills, a struggle between beliefs, and victory goes to the party that crushes the enemy's will and destroys his beliefs.

In other words, the warfare discussed here is a struggle for victory, using "power" to cause the opponent's will to yield and our will to prevail.

Hence, "the essence of warfare" is "power" and its maximum use. Its objective is to crush the opponent's power of resistance and cause him to submit to our will, and its measures are to use power to destroy the opponent's fighting power (material, spiritual). In other words, it is nothing less than the seizure of victory.

b. The essence of warfare and its characteristics

The first essential element of warfare is the fact that, "in warfare, there are opponents." Moreover, both parties are characterized by having free will.

The second is that both parties have the will to overthrow the opponent (enemy). War is a struggle between the free wills of both parties, and victory is determined by which one has confidence in it. In other words, it also can be said to be a struggle of faith.

The third is that power is used to cause submission of the opponent's will. The direct instrument for fighting is "power," and when this power is brought to bear against the opponent, it is used for the violent effect of causing submission of the opponent's will.

The fourth is the actual battlefield situation, which is extremely important for our study of tactics and is a basic condition. The actual battlefield situation arises from the above essential elements of warfare and varies according to the time period, the place of combat, and the type and scale of warfare, etc.

The most important of these are that, in warfare, the situation always is uncertain, unstable, and unclear, and the normal state is that there is a succession of inconsistencies and mistakes, danger to life is ever-present, mental and bodily difficulties of fear, exhaustion, etc., are encountered, the situation does not develop as expected, etc.

In the study of the principles of war and in the study of tactics, if thorough consideration is not always given to the actual battlefield, one will end up in worthless speculation.

2. Characteristics of land warfare

a. In warfare, the essential role of land warfare (land operations) is the control of persons, and its instrument is the control of land.

Hence, the sphere of activity of land units is the land, and the characteristics of the land are the dominant factors governing the character of land warfare. Progress in science and technology contributes greatly to liberation from various limitations of the land, but has not reached the point of changing the basic nature of land warfare.

Also, in the operational environment of land warfare, there are various conditions that affect the handling of troop units and the will of the commander. The principal factors comprising these are national policy (politics, foreign relations, the economy, military affairs, social psychology, etc.), the zone of operations, opposing (enemy) forces, weapon systems, etc., but in this book are treated primarily only matters related to the principles of land-warfare tactics.

   b.  Natural characteristics of the land and their effect

The major elements in the natural characteristics of the land are terrain and weather. It is clear that terrain and weather are closely related to land warfare and that they control the nature of land warfare, but here the discussion is on the general characteristics; special characteristics of terrain and their effect are discussed in Part VII, Operations in Special Terrain, etc.

      (1)  Terrain, particularly the complexity and diversity of the
           surface of the earth

The land forms varied and distinctive terrain (regions) that combines various elements of topographic irregularity, the nature of the surface soil, the water system, the vegetation, cultural features, etc., and exerts great influence on land warfare. This effect, in the final analysis, is related to firepower and tactical movement; but it is not limited simply to physical influence, but also exerts great spiritual influence.

This effect, through field of view and of fire, trajectory, cover and concealment, ability to withstand bombs and shells, etc., aids or limits the use or effectiveness of firepower, and through the load-bearing capacity of the ground, obstructions, etc., favors or curtails the use of tactical mobility.

      (2)  Effect of weather

The amount of light, rain and snow, wind, temperature, etc., are related to the circumstances of the ground surface and affect firepower and tactical mobility, as well as exerting a close influence on the combat capability of personnel and the performance of equipment.

   c.  Characteristics of land warfare

      (1)  Characteristics of employment of land units

         (a) Sluggishness and the fixed nature of operations

Because of the necessity for an uninterrupted link between the base of operations and the battle front and the sluggishness of movement, the shifting and concentration of combat power, change of direction of operations, etc., are sluggish. In land warfare, special consideration is necessary regarding the "importance of a unit," depending upon the unit's size.

         (b)  A region's absorption of combat power

Extending the battle line invites a gradual decrease in combat power (personnel, materiel) because of maintaining of logistics, holding of terrain, etc., and is an important condition making the difference between the offensive and defensive.

(c) Increase in combat capability from the terrain

The value of terrain itself and of fortifications creates the possibility of defense or creates value as an attack objective.

(d) Enduring quality of combat power

The combat power of ground forces--except in cases of panic, the concentration of crushing force, etc.--does not collapse suddenly.

(e) The value of spiritual power is great

With the individual on the battlefield, the mental process at every instant governs the behavior of his entire body. In particular, the value of command and control is extremely high.

(f) Local independence in military operations (combat)

Military operations of large units also have an integrated character of combat in each independent locality.

(2) Organizational character of ground-force units

(a) Organization of essential elements of combat power into minimal units and the necessity for mass

In order to control a region, it is necessary to control localities. In order to organize the control of these localities, there arises the need for various types of firepower and equipment and various branches of service based in small units. And with the naturally limited, small numbers of elite troops, mass is necessary.

(b) Variety of mobile equipment and necessity for mass

Depending upon distance, or depending upon the characteristics of varied terrain to be traversed on foot, mobile equipment of various types and mass are required.

(c) Complexity and expanding nature of the logistical organization

In land warfare, logistics extends from the country's base of operations to the individual fighting man, and with operational conditions becoming complex and varied, expansion of the battle area, modernization of equipment, etc., its organization is complex and expanding. [End of subparagraph (c).]

In a word, the characteristics of land warfare are the source of the principles of war in land warfare, and in order to understand the principles of war, it is necessary to grasp the characteristics of land warfare.

## Chapter III.  Meaning and Nature of the Principles of War

### 1.  What are the principles of war?

The principles of war are "the basic principles of combat in order to obtain victory and the fundamental rules that, to some degree, embody those principles." These are theories and are derived from many military histories.  In other words, "the principles of war are theories formed dialectically from accumulated reasoning and corroborative evidence, and they are continually evolving with the passage of time."  Hence, the principles of war discussed in this book were obtained up to about the end of World War II and cannot be described as unchanging for all times including the future or for all places.

However, when consideration is limited to matters of definite time and space, it is believed that the principles of war discussed in this book can be taken as principles and rules for victory.  On the other hand, in the present situation where the importance of indirect aggression is increasing, one must not overlook the fact that the principles of war or World War II and earlier are reaching a developmental stage.

Also, in one sense, the principles of war are a standard for observing military history and cannot be applied directly in future situations.  Only after knowing the principles of war, carefully studying and observing military history with them as a standard, and then improving one's capability (judgment) through applied tactics, etc., can one tackle situations and make accurate decisions.  Only at that stage can it be said that the principles of war are completely usable.

### 2.  Relationship between the principles of war and doctrines

Doctrines are the guiding principles and the embodiment of basic rules for action that should be taken to embody and carry out national defense policies determined on the basis of the organization and equipment of the country's military forces, national character, traditions, terrain, etc., in the country's environment, that is, in the specific geographic, political, and social conditions.

Thus, although doctrines are not blindly observed, they must at least be followed.  On the other hand, the principles of war are not applied directly but normally are a standard that should be used to improve one's judgment, not something that one should take along during tactical actions.  In other words, doctrines are the direct basis for action, whereas the principles of war are an indirect thing and are put to use in military actions only through assimilation (improving one's power of judgment) by means of normal training applying them.

The relationship between the principles of war and doctrines may be shown graphically as follows:

```
┌─ ─ ─ ─ ─ ─ ─ ─ ─ ─ ─ ─ ─ ─┐
┌──────────────┐            ┌──────────────┐   ┌──────────────┐   ┌──────────────┐
│ Principles   │  Prin-     │ Observation  │   │ Training     │   │Confronting   │
│ (e.g., the   │  ciples    │ and careful  │   │ through      │   │a situation   │
│ superior wins│            │ study of     │   │ applied      │   │that must     │
│ the inferior │  of        │ military     │   │ tactics      │   │be dealt      │
│ loses)       │            │ history      │   │              │   │with          │
└──────────────┘            ├──────────────┤   ├──────────────┤   ├──────────────┤
│ Embodiment   │  war       │ Understanding│   │ Improve-     │   │ Accurate     │
┌──────────────┐            │ and assimila-│   │ ment in      │   │ estimate     │
│ Basic rules  │            │ tion of the  │   │ capability   │   │ of the       │
│ (e.g., the nine│          │ principles   │   │ (judgment)   │   │ situation    │
│ basic rules of │          │ of war       │   │              │   │              │
│ land warfare)│            └──────────────┘   └──────────────┘   └──────────────┘
└──────────────┘
```

Embodiment
in conformity
with the im-
plementation
of national-
defense
policies*

Improvement in tactical capability

┌──────────────┐                    ┌──────────────────┐
│  Doctrine    │ ─────────────────► │ Criteria for action │ = = = ┘
└──────────────┘                    └──────────────────┘

*National-defense policies determined on the basis of the country's specific
geographic, political, and social conditions, the organization and equipment
of that country's armed forces, national character, traditions, terrain, etc.

Fig. 1.  Relationship between the principles of war and doctrines

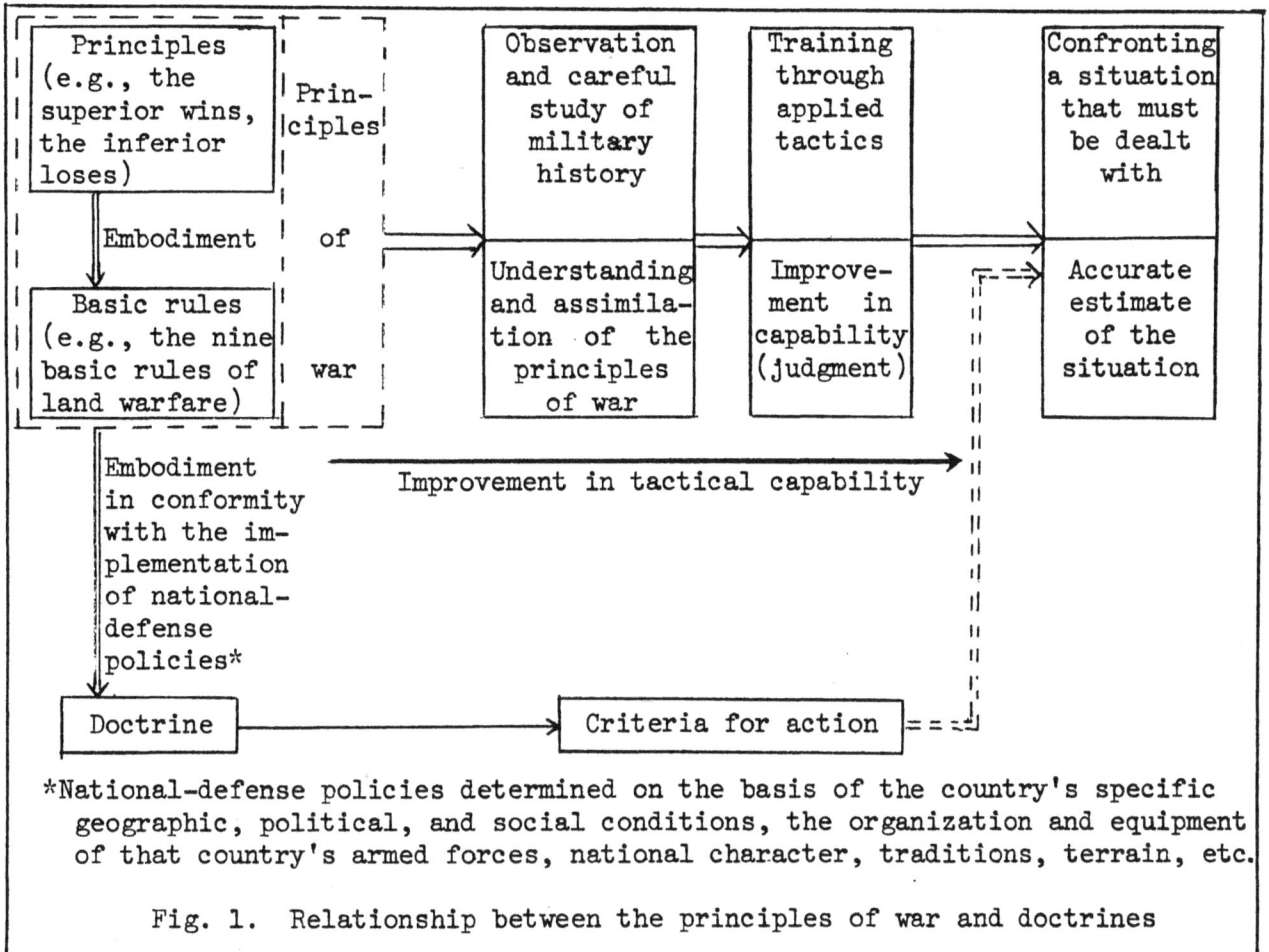

Part II.   MEANING AND CHARACTERISTICS OF COMBAT POWER

Chapter I.   Meaning and Basic Principles of Combat Power

1.  The three factors of combat

Combat is governed by the following three factors:

     ENERGY [POWER]--basic factor in striking the enemy

     TIME--the natural phenomena of light and darkness, heat and cold, fair
         and rainy weather, etc., and timeliness

     SPACE--character of the terrain and other natural phenomena, the spatial
         extent, and posture

These three elements are mutually interrelated and either strengthen or weaken
energy, which is the essence of combat, and whenever energy is applied, they all
are inseparably involved.

Even with the present developments in science and technology, the mutual relationship of these three factors continues unchanged; and among these three elements, energy is most easily changed by manpower and is the factors that must be given most attention for combat.

2. Combat power

War is a struggle between two parties that have free will; and this struggle is an act of violence employed to cause the opponent to submit, and to realize our will. In other words, among the three factors of combat, energy is the direct instrument for combat, and this fighting energy--energy to fight the enemy in military combat--is combat power. Also, with changes in the times, the importance of combat power is gradually increasing, and the proportional difference in importance between it and the factors of time and space is becoming greater and greater.

Combat power is divided into intangible factors and tangible factors.

  a.  Intangible factors

The intangible factors are the mental and bodily capabilities of the individuals and groups that comprise the military units (forces), the most important one being the spiritual strength of the units and forces. In other words, these factors include the following:

    Quality of command and control

    State of discipline (troop morale) and fighting spirit

    Quality of training

    Esprit de corps and the spirit of teamwork

The characteristics of these intangible factors are as follows:

    (1)  Their power (action) is not manifested as a definite quantity and, except in actual combat, cannot be demonstrated even experimentally.

    (2)  They change greatly, depending on people and conditions. In other words, if things go well, multiplied power is brought to bear, but if things go badly, they act as a large minus.

    (3)  They comprise an indivisible unity with the tangible factors and are basic factors that determine victory.

    (4)  The capability of the commander exerts enormous influence on the quality of the spiritual factor of his unit.

  b.  Tangible factors

The tangible factors are the number of persons (military personnel strength) and the quantity and quality of materiel. For example, they are the organization and equipment and the performance, power, and quantities of various weapons; and they are used as casualty-producing power, destructive power, tactical mobility, and other physical strengths.

Tangible factors, to some extent, can be considered as standards with numerical values, and they are the basis for combat power.

3. Principles of combat power

    a. Essence of combat power

Combat power is the basic one of the three factors of combat and, over time and space, changes quickly and continuously.

Combat power, essentially, has four properties. These are the four properties of concentration, dispersion, action, and inaction.

> "Concentration"--Combat power, when concentrated, is strengthened.

> "Dispersion"--Combat power, when dispersed, is weakened.

> "Action"--Combat power, when it takes action, is strengthened.

> "Inaction"--Combat power, when it remains inactive, is weakened.

In other words, combat power, through application and combination of these four properties, brings its character to bear. No matter how much combat power there is, if it is dispersed or remains inactive, that combat power cannot be fully realized, and only when it is concentrated and takes action is the entire combat power used.

From this, when an attempt is made to strike the enemy, the principles of war of "concentration" x "action" result and, hence, the attack is the best means to secure the initiative and be able to obtain decisive results.

The strength and size of combat power are definitely basic conditions for victory, but understanding the nature of combat power and using it skilfully also are essential conditions for victory. It should be remembered that there is an unbroken list of examples since antiquity of disastrous defeats from mistakes in applying the principles of war while having strong and large combat power.

    b. Characteristics of the application of combat power

Items about which caution is necessary in using combat power and in further increasing it, thought out from the three factors of combat and from the nature of combat power, yield the following characteristics:

    (1) Multiplication quality

Combat power, multiplied by various factors, is applied and used against the enemy. In other words, combat power, with appropriate selection and combination of its four properties, is further multiplied by the advantages of time (use of weather, seizing tactical opportunities, etc.) and land (use of terrain, favorable posture, etc.), and only then is it applied as counter-enemy power. Aiming for these multiplied results is an art, and combat power is greatly increased by art.

Application of combat power = (basic combat power) x

$$\underbrace{(\text{selection and combination of its four properties}) \times (\text{time}) \times (\text{space})}_{\text{Art}}$$

### (2) Relativity

In combat, there is always an opponent, and the application of combat power is relative to the enemy, so that there is no basis to be able to show a standard or limit of power that is considered sufficient. Since it is not known whether the enemy will apply power greater than the power we consider optimum, it is necessary conscientiously to muster all factors to the maximum.

### (3) Absoluteness

In cases where the various elements related to the use of combat power exert an effect of approximately the same amount in both forces, victory is in direct proportion to the absolute values of tangible combat power.

As already stated, combat power is a multiplication of tangible and intangible factors, but there clearly are limitations to compensating for deficiencies in tangible factors, that is, principally, the physical combat power, by means of intangible factors, that is, principally the spiritual strength of the unit (force). In other words, in cases where there is more than some given limit of difference between physical combat powers, it is clear that physical combat power cannot be compensated for, even by spiritual strength or strategem.

Here is a principle of war concerning the absoluteness of tangible combat power in the application of combat power.

Note: If D-year is the year in which hostilities commence, the number of years is indicated on the horizontal axis, and combat power on the vertical axis, then the physical-combat-power curve rises sharply after the outbreak of hostilities, whereas the rise of the spiritual-combat-power curve is extremely slow. If combat power is the result of multiplying the two items together, as against a country with a strong rate of increase of physical combat power, no matter how much effort is made to develop spiritual combat power, the outcome is clear.

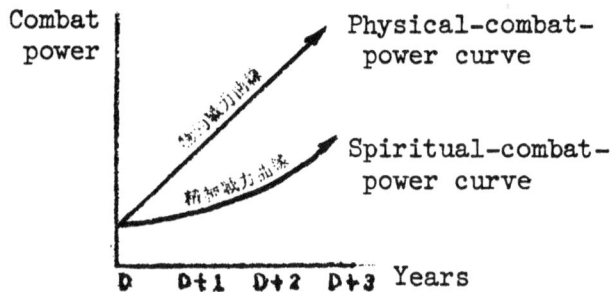

Fig. 2

### (4) Three-dimensionality

When combat power is applied three-dimensionally in the three dimensions of land, sea, and air, it can be largest and most complete.

The three-dimensional nature of combat power makes possible simultaneous neutralization or defense of the entire depth.

When land, sea, and air power is applied in a balance that suits the situation, it is strongest, and air superiority strengthens the ground sphere of dominant power and the control of the sea.

<u>Historical example</u>:  The historical example of the British forces at Sinzweya in the Akyab Campaign in Burma [1944]

     (5)  Weakening

A moving force is gradually weakened by attrition and finally comes to a standstill.  In a way similar to this principle, combat power also is gradually weakened by movement.

In other words:

     (a)  Combat power, with a rapid advance, becomes weaker and, on reaching the combat-power change-about point [where the balance shifts to favor the opponent], comes to a standstill.

     (b)  Confusion produced by the first impact of attack calms down with the passage of time, and the terror effect decreases with the passage of time.

     (c)  The fighting spirit of the attacker is heightened by the intensity of power, being highest at the time of initial impact, and gradually weakens from enemy resistance.

Hence, it is necessary that combat power advance in a way that maintains increasing speed; and for this purpose, it is necessary to dispose combat power in depth.

<u>Historical examples</u>:

    One of the causes for the failure of the offensive of the German forces on the Western Front at the beginning of World War I (insufficient combat power in depth at important fronts).

    Example of the Japanese forces in the Imphal Campaign

    (6)  Directionality

     (a)  Direction of strike by combat power

Strong  Weak

Power

Fig. 3

When power is applied perpendicularly [relative to the enemy], is it strongest physically.  In Cases of oblique directions, power becomes divided, dispersed, and weakened.

Hence, the direction of orientation of combat power must be perpendicular to the enemy.

### (b) Point toward which combat power is directed

If the point toward which combat power is directed is a place where enemy power is superior or equal [to ours], success cannot be expected; and it is necessary that direction be toward a point where enemy power is weak, a point that hinders the action of the enemy's (concentration x action), or a place that requires time for (concentration x action).

Hence, as the element to be attacked, the choice is, firstly, the enemy's rear; secondly, the enemy's flank; thirdly, the outer portion of the enemy's wing; and only if unavoidable, it is necessary to select the front.

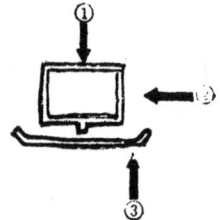

Fig. 4

### (7) Creationality

Combat power is created by people. In other words, it is created and improved while functioning in time and space and is applied on the battlefield to determine victory or defeat with the enemy. The commander's creation of combat power is one of the arts. The commander must be a great artist.

Historical example: The concentration of power by the German forces' combining their air force and armored units at the beginning of World War II.

### (8) Timing

In operations, generally, both sides are in action. These actions change from inaction to action, from concentration to dispersion, or the reverse. The occasions that cause these changes of action are weaknesses; and, with the passage of time, these weaknesses usually gradually become strengths.

## Chapter II. Organizing and Coordinating Combat Power

### 1. Meaning of organizing combat power

The organizing of combat power is the organizing and coordinating of combat power; strictly speaking, it is coordinating for effective application and is a measure indispensable for applying combat power. In other words, only by effectively organizing and coordinating is it possible to apply integrated and sufficient power.

In modern warfare, with the increase in factors comprising combat power and with progress in science and technology, the importance of the effort to organize combat power becomes ever greater.

Command in war, in one viewpoint, can be said to be determining the time and direction for use of combat power, organizing and coordinating combat power, advancing combat power, and maintaining combat power. Among these, organizing and coordinating combat power occupy an important segment of the field of command.

2. Cautionary items in organizing combat **power**

    a.  Fulfilling conditions for application of integrated combat power

For this purpose, firstly, unity of command is an absolute prerequisite.  Since organization is integration in order to achieve effectiveness, if the central point [of command] is absent or multiple, organization itself becomes impossible.

In Operation "Overlord," which is said to have greatly shown the influence of organization, this point was what received attention first.

Second is unity of the plan or concept.  In order to cope with the innumerable changes in battlefield conditions, the initial organizing of combat power estimates changes in the situation and is made with certain assumptions.  In this case, when there is disunity in plan and inconsistency in concept, with development of the tactical situation, organization immediately becomes confused, and coordination collapses.

Hence, unity of command and of plan or concept is extremely important for integrating combat power and for the attainment of common objectives.

Historical example:  Operation "Overlord" of the Allied forces in World War II.

    b.  Complete grasp of the characteristics of the combat power inherent in a unit

In organizing units, it is necessary to understand each [characteristic] correctly and to cause the concentration of the individual characteristics in the most effective manner for the objective.  Command also can be called the road to grasping and combining the individual factors [time, space, power].  An inherent weakness of organization and coordination is that the interruption or deterioration of the action of one of the factors endangers the application of the entire combat power.  Hence, organizing on the basis of inaccurate factors eventuates in no power.

    c.  Originality and surprise

In organizing, there are basic rules, but their form is infinitely varied.  It is devising these forms that is the art of war, and it is this improved originality that favors victory over the enemy.

Historical examples:

    Nobunaga's use of muskets in the Battle of Nagashino [1575]

    Wedge tactics of the German forces

    Island-hopping strategy of the U.S. Armed Forces

    d.  Flexibility

On the battlefield with its innumerable changes, rejection of rigid organization and successive shifts in flexible organization and coordination through flexible thinking, constitute the cardinal principle of command and the basis of success. For this reason, it always is necessary to prepare reserve plans or to formulate supplementary measures, etc., as counterplans to meet changes in the situation.

Coordination must be careful; it is a continuing process, and when a plan is once established, that does not mean that everything is finished.

Historical example:  Tactics of Soviet forces at Nomonhan (at first, the Soviet forces rushed tanks to the front, meeting the counterattack of the Japanese forces; thereafter, it used dummy tanks and, after neutralizing exposed positions Japanese forces by means of artillery, applied the combined combat power of infantry combat, achieving success).

    e.  Not presenting openings that the enemy can take advantage of

Not leaving openings is not only rational and effective, but also means strength against enemy counterattacks.

For example, the U.S. Navy's circular formation, Germany's Panzerfaust (moving fortress) in World War II, the British-type circular position at Sinzweya in the Second Akyab Campaign, the circular defensive position of the U.S. and Chinese forces in the Hukawng Valley at the northern border of Burma, etc., are good typical examples.

    f.  Timeliness in meeting the situation

The accuracy and flexibility of organization increase in direct proportion to the time, and tactical opportunities and coordination are opposites.

The elapse of time for organization increases combat power but may miss a valuable tactical opportunity.

It is necessary to decide between time (opportunity) and power by proper appraisal of enemy power, of the necessity for organizing our combat power, and of the constraints of time.

For example, in case of an attack, the question arises of whether to coordinate and go with power or to seize the tactical opportunity and go with art.  If too much importance is placed on the tactical opportunity and an attack is initiated with insufficient power, the attack will suddenly bog down.

Hence, it is important to grasp this limitation.  Ascertaining necessary power and integrating that with the time requirement, results in the organizing of maximum combat power.

Historical examples:

    Examples of success in organizing combat power:

        Normandy landing operation

        "Cylindrical" defense at Sinzweya [encircled but with aerial supply]

Examples of failure in organizing combat power:

Counterattacks of Gallipoli, Guadalcanal, and Saipan

## Chapter III. Tactical Opportunity and the Surprise Attack

### 1. Relative combat power

Combat power, as already stated, is applied by the multiplication of various factors. Hence, it is self-evident that differences will occur in the power actually applied on the battlefield, irrespective of the intrinsic combat power.

Combat is a relative matter, and both sides, respectively, fight with the power that they actually can apply. The power that both sides, respectively, can apply is called the relative combat power.

The outcome of battle receives its verdict of the superior wins and the inferior loses, on the basis of this relative combat power. All the concrete principles of war that are derived from the basic principle of war that the superior wins and the inferior loses, are simply the seeking of the cause-and-effect relationship of how to create and improve relative combat power superior to that of the enemy.

Comparison of the power of both sides in the study of tactics is not merely a ratio of firepower or of military-personnel strength; superiority must be evaluated based on this relative combat power.

In combat, for us to have superiority in relative combat power, every effort must be concentrated on utilization of terrain and weather, establishment of a favorable posture, obtaining pertinent intelligence, logistic support, etc.; but the most important tactic is utilization of tactical opportunity and the surprise attack.

### 2. Tactical opportunity

   a. Meaning of tactical opportunity

Tactical opportunity is the chance of victory.

In other words, it is an inevitable or chance opportunity in war where we can expect superiority in our relative combat power (our application of combat power sufficient to be able to defeat or destroy the enemy).

Also, tactical opportunity is a continually shifting thing. The tactical opportunity normally lasts only a short time, this differing with the size of the unit. Some last only a moment, some continue for some time. Also, there are tactical opportunities that occur not just once but several times.

b.  How does a favorable combat opportunity arise?

   (1)  Created by one's own effort

For example,

   (a)  Luring the enemy into terrain where one's own combat power can
        be used but application of enemy combat power is difficult.

   (b)  Trapping the enemy into a situation where his combat personnel
        are split.

   (c)  Acting so that our posture is favorable to us.

In other words, it is causing the enemy to expose his weak points, in judo
called "preparatory action and attack" (breaking the opponent's posture, creating a posture where a throw is easily effected, and oneself effecting the throw).

   (2)  Occurring by chance during the course of combat or occurring as a
        result of waiting

Examples include the following:

   (a)  Splitting of enemy combat personnel, confusion, carelessness,
        etc., resulting from the enemy's mistakes.

   (b)  Deficiency in the enemy's application of combat power because
        of the effect of terrain and weather.

   (c)  Seizing the point of termination of an enemy offensive (combat-
        power change-about point).

c.  Use of the tactical opportunity

A tactical opportunity must be grasped and used.

For this reason, if the commander gathers timely, appropriate intelligence information, detects a tactical opportunity through discerning foresight and an
eye for opportunity, and, at some time, seizes a tactical opportunity, this must
be utilized through excellent decisiveness and executive ability.

At that time, within some limit, it is possible to change even numerical inferiority into superior relative combat power through utilization of a tactical opportunity, but for this purpose, it always is necessary to make appropriate
preparations in order to be able to seize the tactical opportunity, and particular care must be taken not to jump uselessly at an opportunity, attack without
preparation, and be defeated.

Also, it is important for commanders of all ranks to stress quick and alert
command, the will to seize opportunities, and independent, aggressive action.

<u>Historical examples:</u>

Examples of success in seizing tactical opportunities:

Battle of Shizugatake (army of Hideyoshi Hashiba [=Toyotomi])[1583]

Inchon Landing in the Korean War [1950]

Example of failure in seizing tactical opportunities:

Battle of Yamazaki (army of Mitsuhide Akechi)[1582]

3. Tactic of mass

a. Meaning of the tactic of mass

The tactic of mass is the concentration of an overwhelmingly large quantity of military manpower and materiel and the formation of combat power with absolute superiority in quantity over that of the enemy.

For the Soviet forces, evolving this mass tactic is an essential condition of combat, and in the German-Soviet struggle in World War II, the German forces were crushed by this tactic.

b. Relationship between tactical opportunity and mass

In military history from ancient times on, there are many examples of compensating for inferior mass through utilizing a tactical opportunity and seizing victory, but in cases where there is a great difference in mass, it is difficult for the inferior to obtain a superior position in relative combat power, regardless of his effort to utilize tactical opportunities.

It is difficult to indicate by figures the difference in mass that can be compensated for, by utilizing a tactical opportunity, but it can be said that the inferior side cannot win against an enemy that has more than some given limit in absolute superiority in mass.

Also, it must be noted that a unit that emphasizes tactical opportunities, once it has missed a tactical opportunity, will experience great impact when a tactical opportunity is seized by the enemy; and on the other hand, a unit that emphasizes the tactic of mass, when mass is lost, also will experience great impact.

4. Surprise attack

a. Meaning of surprise attack

Surprise attack is attempting to gain superiority in relative combat power by taking the enemy unawares and not giving the enemy time to react.

Here it must be noted that, even if it is possible to effect a surprise at first, when the enemy, by taking countermeasures, is in a superior position in relative combat power, it is not a surprise attack but merely effecting a surprise. On the other hand, in cases where superiority in relative combat power is retained by a swift and daring sudden strike that does not give the enemy time to take countermeasures, that can be called a surprise attack. In short, not giving the enemy time for counteraction is of primary importance for a surprise attack, and for this reason, power and speed are necessary. The principle of war of surprise attack rests on this.

<u>Note</u>:  Increase in power through strategem:

    Emphasizing strategem......surprise attack

    Emphasizing power.........assault

    From strategem x power.....sudden attack

    (The term "surprise attack" in current manuals may be said to be a general term for all three.)

    b.  Types of surprise attack

There are various types of measures and methods for achieving a surprise attack, but these may be classified by form, as follows:

    (1)  Time-type surprise attack

    (2)  Place-type surprise attack

    (3)  Mass-type surprise attack

    (4)  Quality-type surprise attack

    (5)  Tactics-type surprise attack

All of these are achieved by use of terrain and weather, application of speed, concealment and deception, change of measures and methods, etc.

    c.  Effectiveness of the surprise attack

The effectiveness of the surprise attack is, firstly, destruction of the enemy's intangible combat power through spiritual impact, that is, aiming at confusion of command, lowered morale, etc., and secondly, through our swift strike, making difficult the application of the enemy's tangible combat power (personnel, weapons, etc.).

In other words, it is an attempt, by combining these two elements, to curtail greatly the application of the enemy's combat power and to gain superiority for our relative combat power.

Historical examples:

    Time-type surprise attack:

        Battle of Okehazama [1560]

        Landing of U.S. forces on Saipan and Guadalcanal

    Place-type surprise attack:

        Battles of Ichinotani [1184] and Itsukushima [1555]

        Napoleon's crossing of the Alps

    Tactics-type surprise attack:

        Battle of Nagashino [1575]

        Blitz operations of the German Army in World War II

    Technological-type surprise attack

        Appearance of tanks in the [Battle of the] Somme [1916]

        Atomic bomb

        Chapter IV.  Frontal Combat Power and Combat Power in Depth

1.  Meaning of frontal combat power

Frontal combat power is each unit's combat power directed toward the front
facing the enemy in order to accomplish a battle role.  In other words, along
with deploying first-line manpower on its own battle front and applying its own
combat power, each unit is supported by artillery and aviation firepower and, if
necessary, is reinforced with airborne troops and heliborne forces, and it also
is directed three-dimensionally, air-defense combat power being directed against
the enemy's air power.

The question of how much manpower to assign to the first line differs according
to mission, terrain, enemy situation, degree of firepower support, etc.  Considered in isolation, the greater the manpower density, the greater the combat
power; but on the other hand, in cases of density exceeding some definite limit,
combat power is decreased.  Hence, a manpower density favorable to the application of combat power generally remains within a definite range.

2.  Significance and necessity of combat power in depth

In order to gain victory, superiority in combat power must be applied continuously and with suitable width and depth not only in the initial period but until
achievement of the goal (seizing the objective), and the enemy must be kept under strong pressure throughout.  Also, since first-line manpower suffers attrition rapidly with the progress of combat with the enemy, in order to maintain
it, continuous and uninterrupted replacement of combat power is necessary.  In

this way, combat power maintained in depth in order continually to apply maximum frontal combat power and to maintain and improve it, is combat power in depth.

On the other hand, maintenance of combat power in depth may generate a doubt as to whether there may not occur the mistake of piecemeal use of combat power, but this will not necessarily occur.

This is because the gains achieved by the first-line units are immediately utilized and expanded by units in the rear, so that the initial attack shock effect remains undiminished. In this case, if the opportunity is missed to utilize the gains of the first line, there is slippage into piecemeal use of combat power. Hence, selection of the opportunity and of the appropriate position to introduce combat power in depth and application of tactical mobility are important conditions.

Historical example:  Battle of Mikata-ga-hara

At Mikata-ga-hara, Ieyasu Tokugawa was present with a [latent] "inverted wedge" formation as in the sketch map, whereas Shingen Takeda deployed all his units in depth and fought by means of the tactic of "rotating elements in the fighting line." As a result, Ieyasu's force initially was superior, but gradually was overcome by the combat power of Shingen's force deployed in depth; and the fact that, in the end, victory fell to Takeda's force is a good example showing the importance of maintaining combat power in depth.

The caution in Sun-tzu, "in communicating-ground [=terrain equally accessible to both forces] do not allow your formations to become separated," also is this principle.

Fig. 5.  Map of the Battle of Mikata-ga-hara 22 Dec 1572

3.  Maintenance of combat power in depth

    a.  Maintenance of combat power in depth is dependent on echelonned distribution of combat power and on reserves.
Note:  Here, reserves is not only reserve troops but also includes all the combat power of firepower, logistics, etc.

    b.  Echelonned distribution of combat power, for example, division into first- and second-line assault units in the assault and into first- and second-line defense units in the defense, has the sole objective of applying combat power in depth.

    c.  The mission of reserves is to maintain combat power in depth and to cope with unexpected situations, and they should be used to the maximum in the application of combat power in depth. At that time, concentrated use at critical times and places is important.

4. The battle front and distribution in depth
   Note:  Distribution in depth means the distribution in depth of combat power
          in order to constitute combat power in depth.

The battle front and distribution in depth are inseparably related.

It resembles, for example, the relation between width and
depth in quadrilaterals of the same area.  In other words,
with a given combat power, if the battle front is increased, distribution in depth is decreased, and if distribution in depth is increased, the battle front is
decreased.  This correlation is extremely important.

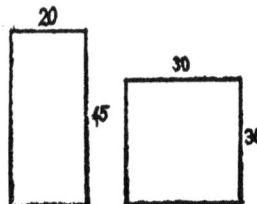

The items that should be considered in determining the
battle front and distribution in depth, may be listed as
follows:

Fig. 6

   a.  Adapting width and depth to the objective to be achieved (objective to
       be seized)

   b.  Power in the spearhead exceeding that of the enemy

   c.  Flank-support relationship

   d.  The enemy's situation, particularly the front and depth

   e.  Terrain and weather

Chapter V.  Containment and Strike

1. The 4F principles in combat

Combat involves the following four functions:

   a.  Find     (Intelligence function)

   b.  Fix      (Containment action)

   c.  Fight    (Strike action)

   d.  Finish   (Achieving the battle success)

Of these, the main element is the third, strike action, and success in this is
an annihilation battle.

2. Relationship between containment and strike

   a.  In order to crush (strike) enemy combat power by means of our combat
power, the primary condition is the place struck by the enemy's combat power;
and for this reason, it is clear that action is necessary that contains enemy
combat power to our desired time and place.  Thus, containment and the strike
have a close and inseparable relationship.

b. Two types of sequences of containment and strike action may be considered, as follows:

    (1) The case of first containing the enemy and then effecting the strike

    (2) The case of accomplishing the continment and strike simultaneously

Both cases are the same in their relation to the essential nature of containment action, which is "impeding (limiting) the enemy's freedom of action."

c. Containment actions necessary for the strike include the following:

    (1) Impeding the movement of combat power

    (2) Impeding the organization (reorganization) of combat power

    (3) Impeding the change of speed of combat power

    (4) Impeding or forcing change of direction of combat power

3. Examples of applying containment and the strike [Numbers in quotation marks are keyed to the respective figures]

    a. Attack

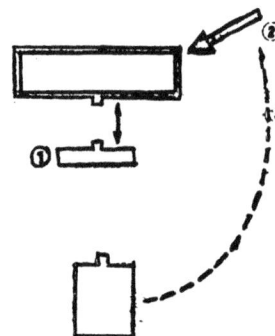

Fig. 7

      (1) Envelopment and turning movement [Fig. 7]

        "1" Containment of the enemy on his front

        "2" Moving to a favorable position and striking

      (2) Breakthrough [Fig. 8]

        "1" Containment (impeding movement) by a secondary attack

        "2" Strike by the main attack

    b. Defense [Fig. 9]

      "1" Blocking of the enemy by positions, interdiction of reinforcement by firepower (containment)

      "2" Counterattack by reserves (strike)

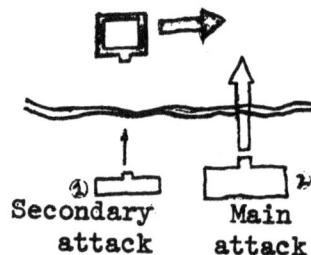

Secondary attack    Main attack

Fig. 8

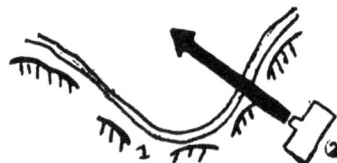

Fig. 9

c. Pursuit [Fig. 9]

"1" Unit assigned to exert direct pressure....containment of enemy withdrawal by continuous and unrelenting pressure

"2" Unit assigned to a turning movement....interdicting the enemy's route of withdrawal and encircling and destroying the enemy (strike)

d. Defense against amphibious landings

Coastal-defense [large-unit] group (containment) and strike [large-unit] group (strike).

## Part III.  CONCENTRATION OF COMBAT POWER

### Chapter I.  Summary

1. Significance of concentration of combat power

a. Meaning of "concentration of combat power"

"Concentration of combat power" is the assembling of as much as possible of our combat power and its integrated application at critical times and places.

This is one of the "methods of using power" that apply limited power in the most effective manner and one of the most important principles of war derived from the basic principle of war that superiority wins and inferiority loses.

b. Why is "concentration of combat power" one of the most important principles of war?

"Concentration of combat power" makes it possible for us to create relative superiority at decisive times and places even though we are inferior in the overall ratio of relative combat power of both sides.

In other words, battle occurs with both sides using limited power in a course of time and space called a battlefield.  Within this time and space, there exists a critical point that also could be called the decisive point, namely, a [specific] time and place.  If victory is gained at that point, even if another unimportant area is temporarily disadvantageous, complete victory can be gained.

c. How should victory be gained at the critical point?

The fact that this can be done by applying superior combat power sufficient to destroy the enemy, is clearly reflected also in the basic principle of war that superiority wins and inferiority loses.

In order for us to gain superiority in the ratio of relative combat power at the decisive time and place, we must not only strive to concentrate combat power but also make a maximum effort to disperse and destroy enemy combat power.

Separating part of the combat power for a supporting operation or secondary attack, at first sight, seems contrary to the concentration of combat power, but it is based on the above concept. The military-personnel strength allocated to this, however, of course, should be the minimum necessary.

   d.  Mistake of piecemeal commitment of combat power

Occurrences that conflict with the concentration of combat power are dispersed commitment and piecemeal commitment of combat power. This relationship, with counterbattery fire of our two [guns] to the enemy's three, may be depicted graphically as follows:

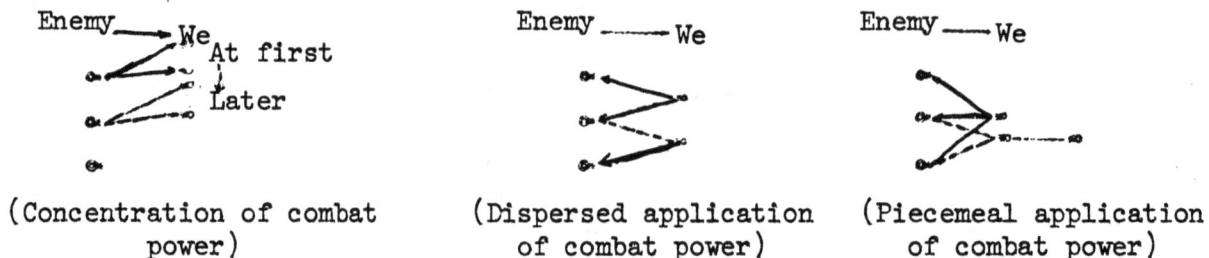

(Concentration of combat          (Dispersed application        (Piecemeal application
        power)                       of combat power)             of combat power)

Figure 10

Dispersed commitment and piecemeal commitment of combat power such as in the above examples, in the light of the basic principle of war that superiority wins and inferiority loses, clearly are major errors, but in actual combat, these errors are easy to make.

The main reasons for this are as follows:

   (1)  Insufficient knowledge of the situation, particularly the enemy situation

   (2)  Deficiency in attention to tactical opportunities and to associated combat power

   (3)  Case of lapsing into a passive posture

Here it must be noted that the error of piecemeal commitment of combat power is basically different from the piecemeal commitment of insufficient military personnel, for example, elements successively entering combat in a meeting engagement.

In regard to elements successively entering combat in a meeting engagement, it must be noted that a necessary condition is to be able to maintain superiority in relative combat power throughout the combat, making rapid attacks on enemy weak points or being able to rely on superiority throughout at key positions in the battle situation that control the battle situation.

2.  Necessary conditions that should be considered for concentrating combat power

    a.  Establishment of objective, and a consistent plan

In the absence of establishment of an objective of the operation and a consistent plan based upon it, as well as of the steadfast and intense will of the commander to carry it out, there will not be effective concentration and application of combat power.

    b.  Positive initiative

A negative, passive posture merely follows the enemy and cannot concentrate combat power.  Since attack is characterized by initiative, concentration of combat power is easy, and this advantage should be applied to the maximum.  Since defense is passive, combat power easily becomes dispersed.  For this reason, particularly at critical times and places, one must actively strive to concentrate combat power.

    c.  Selection of the critical time and place

These are the time and place that determine victory, that is, the decisive point. In concentrating combat power, it is extremely important first to select an appropriate decisive point.  This is not a momentary point, but it has width and depth.  If a mistake is made in this selection, not only does it not link to victory, but also the carefully concentrated combat power will end in a fizzle, and the result will be that the enemy turns our strength to his advantage.  This involves the case of our taking the initiative in action and the case created by the relative relationships of the two sides, but one must act with positive initiative and, in the second case, discernment is necessary to seize tactical opportunities.

In other words, it may be said that the decisive point is a terrain point that produces the "tactical opportunity" mentioned above.

    d.  Integrated application of combat power

Merely assembling combat power superior to that of the enemy is equivalent to a mob.  If combat strength is not organized, not concentrated against a vital part of the enemy (decisive point), and not applied integrally, it is meaningless.

In particular, in modern warfare, it is necessary to concentrate combat power three-dimensionally, of course with integration of ground, sea, and air, and with organic cooperation of all branches of service, and main and secondary attacks, firepower and tactical mobility, front and depth, operations and intelligence, communications, logistics, and other functions must be integrated and organized so as to apply maximum combat power at critical times and places.

Also, for this, there must be continuity over a desired time period and under a consistent plan.

e. Economic use of combat power

Concentration of combat power requires economical use of combat power on other fronts. In other words, in order to apply maximum combat power at the decisive point, along with maximum curtailment of combat power directed to other areas, it is necessary not to create so-called poorly dispositioned troops, so that no element of the combat power would be made idle.

On the other hand, it is necessary to strive for maximum dispersion and destruction of enemy combat power. As stated above, support operations, secondary attacks, etc., are based on this concept and coincide with economical use of combat power. The statement in Sun-tzu that "knowing use of the disparity in numbers is victory," is this principle.

f. Application of tactical mobility

Warfare, considered from one viewpoint, also can be described as a contest by both sides to concentrate combat power against decisive points. In other words, in order to concentrate desired combat power superior to that of the enemy at a desired time and place, application of swift tactical mobility is an essential condition.

In modern warfare, because of advances in science and technology, particularly developments in firepower and tactical mobility, dispersal of military personnel is regarded as extremely important. In other words, dispersion is important from the viewpoint of maintenance of flexibility; of protection, especially reduction of casualties; of concealment of plans, etc.; and excessive concentration at unnecessary times should be avoided as mush as possible.

In other words, the concentration of combat power from a dispersed posture is becoming increasingly important, and for that reason, there must be an effort not merely to use tactical mobility, but also to use mobility of firepower (concentration of fire), reliable command-communications capability, etc.

3. Methods of concentrating combat power

Methods of concentrating combat power are of the following two types:

a. Method of concentrating combat power before arriving on the battlefield (Napoleonic-type concentration method)

Piecemeal defeat of enemy elements by means of concentrated combat power (interior lines)

[Note: numbers in Fig. 11 indicate combat power.]

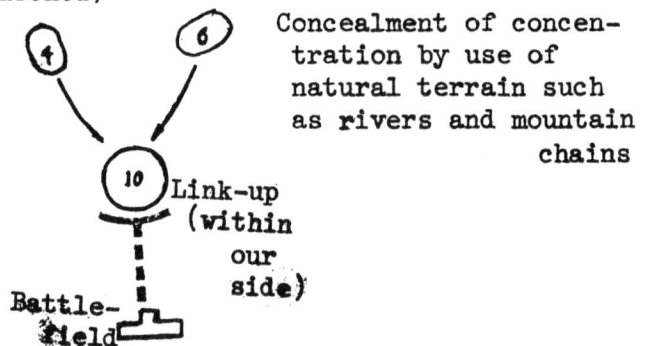

Concealment of concentration by use of natural terrain such as rivers and mountain chains

Fig. 11

b.  Method of concentrating combat
    power on the battlefield (Moltke-
    type concentration method)

Exterior-lines operation

Note:  Numbers [in Fig. 12] indicate
combat power.

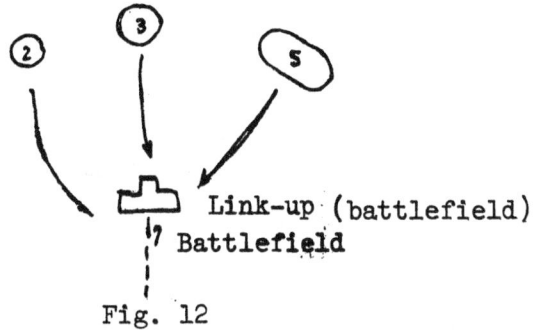

Fig. 12

Link-up (battlefield)
Battlefield

## Historical examples:

Examples of failure to concentrate combat power:

The Soviet Army at the beginning of German-Soviet campaigns [1941]

The drive into North Korea by the United Nations forces in the Korean War

Error of piecemeal commitment of combat power:

The Russian Army in the Russo-Japanese War

Guadalcanal, Leyte, and New Guinea campaigns

Southward advance into North Korea by the People's Republic of China Army in the Korean War

### Chapter II.  Centripetal Use of Combat Power

### Section 1.  Principle of centripetalism

1.  Meaning of centripetalism

Centripetalism is the movement from every point on the circumference of a circle toward its central point, and the principle of centripetalism is the principle of using power in this way.  [Fig. 13]

2.  Characteristics and effectiveness of the use of centripetalism

a.  By use of centripetalism, all power elements moving toward the center are directed toward a common point at the center.

b.  It has the advantage of mutually correlating and concerting all the power elements on the perimeter.  In other words, the effectiveness of power exerted on the central point is larger than the simple total of the individual power elements on the perimeter.

Fig. 13

In the above figure [Fig. 13], power exerted on the center > a + b + c.

c. In regard to the effectiveness of power against the center:

(1) These power elements become greater as they approach the center and are at a maximum when they reach the center.

(2) These power elements are greatest and most effective when they are used simultaneously.

(3) The faster the movement of these power elements, the greater their effectiveness.

3. Application of the principle of centripetalism

The principle of centripetalism, in the posture sphere, is a principle of war of a method of concentrating combat power and, militarily, is applied in operations on exterior lines, advancement in separated columns to link up for combat, envelopment, turning movements, etc.

Also, the characteristic of offensive operations is concentration, and the attack can be said to use centripetalism.

Section 2.   Operations on exterior lines

1. Meaning of operations on exterior lines

a. The operation on exterior lines is an operation that maintains lines of communication outwards and is carried out toward a central point from several directions, against an enemy with operations directed outward.

In other words, from the viewpoint of posture, it is operating from the beginning in a relative position of envelopment or pincer attack against the enemy; and from the viewpoint of the line of operations (axis of operations), it is an operation carried out with the line of operations held on the outer flank of the enemy.

b. The operation on exterior lines is an operation that centripetally concerts separated elements of combat power, the effectiveness of this combat power being concentrated on a single common point, so that it is the operation that makes maximum use of the principle of centripetalism.

From the viewpoint of concentration of combat power, this is an operation that, as stated above, unites separated elements of combat power on the battlefield at a suitable time for operational purposes -- in other words, an operation based on the "Moltke-type concentration method."

c. In the disposition (strategic deployment) and use of combat power in operations on exterior lines, there are the following two methods, shown on the figure at the right:

(1) Method that has each unit "a," "b," "c," disposed on the perimeter attacking an

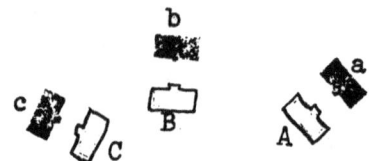

Fig. 14

- 32 -

opposing enemy, and using combat power in a concentrating manner.

(2) Method in which force "a" checks the attack of the superior force "A" and contains that unit, while forces "b" and "c" destroy facing enemy elements and then assault the flanks and rear of force "A," consolidating all combat power and destroying the enemy.

2. Characteristics and results of the operation on exterior lines

a. It is possible to envelop the enemy and to hold and destroy him.

In other words, with the operation on exterior lines, a basic disposition is constituted that is suitable for leading to envelopment; and by its centripetal movement, it naturally is possible to envelop the enemy strategically and tactically.

b. Strategically, it is an extremely advantageous operation.

In other words, the operation on exterior lines is extremely reliable, having the natural benefits of controlling the enemy on its single line of operations and not being controllable by the enemy. Also, if a force operating on interior lines attempts to defeat separately one of the forces operating on exterior lines, its flank or rear is threatened by another force, and crushing enemy forces in detail cannot easily be planned.

In other words, it can be said that a force operating on exterior lines not only can cut the enemy's line of withdrawal but also can threaten the enemy's base of operations and, on the other hand, that a threat against our own rear is almost impossible.

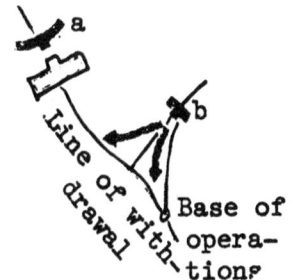

c. The operation on exterior lines is an operation that holds the initiative

The force operating on exterior lines is unrestricted in use of time and space for operations and can hold the initiative in conducting operations. In an operation with no margin of spare time, it is absolutely necessary to seek a quick victory, and the force operating on interior lines loses time and terrain for operations from one moment to the next. Great importance must be given to small pressures from these exterior lines.

Fig. 15

d. The strategy of the superior force is the so-called strategy of the strong

Without a superior force, strategy on exterior lines cannot exist. Hence, if this real power is applied correctly, success will be achieved in many cases.

e. On the other hand, it involves the danger of falling into a splitting of combat power and being subjected to piecemeal defeat of units.

Hence, it is extremely important to select a suitable direction of operations and to cause closely concerted action among all units, to combine all elements of tangible and intangible combat power, and not to give the enemy an opportunity for piecemeal victories.

In summary, the operation on exterior lines is offensive, holds the initiative, seizes the superior posture position, and exerts great centripetal force from all directions. And once the force operating on interior lines has failed to defeat in detail the forces operating on exterior lines, the offensive force naturally is in a posture for strategic envelopment and, ultimately, can effect a complete envelopment tactically.

3. Condition for occurrence of an operation on exterior lines

    a. Geographic relationships of the country (national boundary)

As with Prussia in the Austro-Prussian War and with the Allied forces in World War I and World War II, when forming a posture is necessarily on exterior lines because of geographic relationships, with no leeway for choice between operations on interior and on exterior lines, the determination is natural.

In worldwide great wars, however, interior and exterior lines are unclear and, in many cases, confused. In such cases, it is taken on a larger scale and generalized on the principle of war of the line of communications.

    b. Geographic relationships of the zone of operations

In local operations, selection of disposition of combat power on interior and exterior lines can be made on the basis of the characteristics of the zone of operations, in particular, directions of rivers and mountain chains, the traffic network of roads, railroads, etc., fortifications, etc.

In other words, in the figure below, the Nagoya or Numazu area is a good example of this.

In other words, as to selection of the operational zone, it is necessary to seek an area that will guide the enemy into interior lines, and that will permit us to use the advantage of our exterior lines.

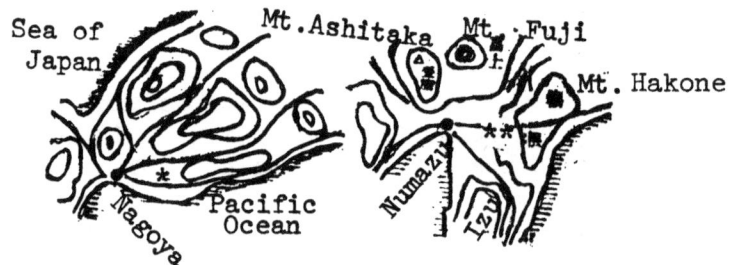

Sea of Japan · Mt.Ashitaka · Mt. Fuji · Mt. Hakone · Pacific Ocean · Nagoya · Numazu · Izu

*Eastern part of     **Mishima
Nobi Plain

    c. Tactical (strategic) conditions

Fig. 16

        (1) Case in which the basic disposition of combat power is dispersed, especially where concentration of combat power is to be in a single area, is even more disadvantageous

An example of this occurred in the Austro-Prussian War of 1866, when Moltke, in order to precede the Austrian Army in concentrating, had his troop strength, that was in a dispersed basic disposition, move to the battlefield in separate columns and link-up there.

(2) Case of being able to change from an interior-lines posture to exterior lines

For example, the case of being able to mount a pursuit operation after exploitation of a success in an attack, or an operation on exterior lines against surviving enemy elements after piecemeal defeat of enemy units.

4. Matters that should be kept in mind in the conduct of operations on exterior lines

The primary aim in the conduct of operations on exterior lines is to expand the initial superiority in posture and the advantage of the initiative, force the enemy into a passive posture, conduct a centripetal operation, and hold and destroy the enemy from the perimeter.

For this purpose, matters that should be kept particularly in mind in connection with the conduct [of operations] are as follows:

a. Quickly constricting the posture on exterior lines and guiding into tactical envelopment

Exterior lines are strategic. They are not, like envelopment, a tactical action.

If it is not a division or larger unit with independent combat power, it does not have the pressure for dispersal and concerted action on exterior lines. Hence, it is a mistake to speak of having a part of a division disposed on exterior lines.

b. Alertness to avoid defeat in detail

It is necessary to ensure cooperation and coordination among all dispersed units, hasten the course of the operation, and preclude piecemeal defeat attempted by the force operating on interior lines.

c. Forces disposed on exterior lines must not forget concentration of combat power

When combat power is dispersed on exterior lines separated by terrain that prevents cooperation, one must not fall into the bad practice of overlooking tactical opportunities to consolidate combat power. On the other hand, we must use cleverness to contain and disperse the enemy over a broad front and to concentrate our combat power in a single area.

d. Attempting to conceal one's plans and making a sudden attack on the enemy

It is necessary to take a suitable direction of operations, keep plans secret, make a sudden attack on the enemy, give the enemy no opening for counteraction, and give no opportunity for piecemeal defeat [of our forces].

Historical examples:

Examples of operations on exterior lines:

In the China Incident [Sino-Japanese War, 1937-1945], the operations of Wuhan, Nanjing [Nanking], Chang-gui [Ch'ang-kuei], and Xuzhou [Hsüchou]

Example of slipping into strength dispersal and being subjected to piecemeal defeat:

Japanese forces in the Imphal Campaign

Examples of shifting from an operation on interior lines to one on exterior lines:

British forces at Imphal

Raising of the sieges of Moscow, Stalingrad, and Leningrad

Section 3. Advancing from different directions and linking up to attack

1. Meaning of advancing from different directions and linking up to attack

Advancing from different directions and linking up to attack, is the maneuver of advancing from several different areas in order to envelop and destroy the enemy, the positioning in separate advances being with a view to combining combat power at a suitable time.

Also, advancing from separate directions and linking up to attack, as a posture, is an operation on exterior lines.

2. Form of advancing from different directions and linking up to attack

The form of advancing from different directions and linking up to attack, is extremely varied according to the direction, time, place, and intervals of the separated advances. Representative examples are as follows:

a. According to direction

(1) From two opposite directions    (2) From three opposing directions

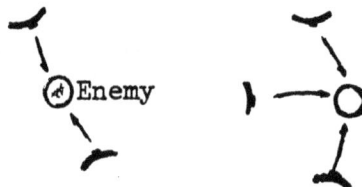

Fig. 17

- 36 -

(3)  From all around        (4)  From several nonopposing directions

Fig. 18

b.  According to disposed posture before the separated advances

   (1)  From initially united posture      (2)  From initially dispersed
                                               posture

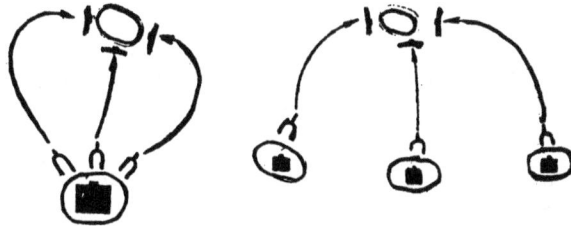

Fig. 19

c.  Accomplished in echelons [Fig. 20]

d.  According to the relationship of distance to
    objective

   (1)  Having approximately equal distances

   (2)  Having substantial differences

Fig. 20

e.  According to the times of separated advance
    and combined attack

   (1)  Times are simultaneous

   (2)  Staggered times

Historical examples:  Examples of advancing from different directions and
linking up to attack:

   Moltke's separated advance with combined attack at Königgrätz in the
   Austro-Prussian War of 1866

   Separated advance with combined attack by the Japanese forces in the Battle
   of Xuzhou [Hsüchou][1938]

   Defeat of the Japanese forces at Imphal

3.  Items that must be taken into consideration in implementation of advancing from different directions and linking up to attack

    a.  Selection of the objective for the combined attack

Ordinarily, there initially is selected a strategic point, that is, a strategic objective, but with development of the operation, a definite objective is determined with the purpose of defeating the enemy or occupying terrain.

The essential goal of advancing from different directions and linking up to attack, is not simply the concentration of combat power, but the link-up of combat power on the battlefield, that is, the envelopment and destruction of the enemy.

Historical examples:

   Battle of Königgrätz.  (The initial objective was Gitschin, merely for concentration of forces, but during the operation, it was changed to Königgrätz for destruction of the enemy.)

   Battle of Liaoyang in the Russo-Japanese War.  (The objective of the Japanese forces in advancing from different directions and linking up to attack, was the strategic objective of Liaoyang, but the strategic objective in the Russian forces' battle plan also was Liaoyang.)

   b.  What should be done to avoid piecemeal defeat by the enemy?

       (1)  Appropriate disposition of combat power for separated advance.

In other words, there must be appropriate selection of the main and secondary operation areas, and allocation of adequate combat power to them.

For this purpose,

           (a)  It is necessary to ensure superiority in relative combat power against expected enemy resistance during the separated advance.

           (b)  Consideration is given to movement distances for the separated advance and to topographic conditions in the area where separated advance occurs.

           (c)  Appropriate allocation of combat power in the link-up area is made, with consideration of enemy counteraction, terrain conditions, our operational goals, etc.

       (2)  Achieving close cooperation among the elements of combat power that are advancing separated.

For this purpose, it is necessary to achieve appropriate direction of operations and to exercise appropriate time and space controls.

(3) Allocation of the terrain and routes of separated advance in such a way. as to be suitable for mutual support of separately advancing elements of combat power.

(4) Maintaining suitable tactical mobility for separately advancing units, and using speed of movement that does not give the enemy time for counteraction

(5) Giving severe attention to keeping the plan secret and achieving the results of a surprise attack.

c. Superiority of relative combat power (striking power) in the final stage

As stated earlier, separated advance from different directions and linking up to attack is a means and not a goal. Hence, it is very important to retain striking power to envelop and destroy the enemy in the final stage.

For this purpose, it is necessary to be careful to effect three-dimensional envelopment that interdicts the withdrawal route not only by separately advancing combat power from land routes but also by naval and air combat power, and it is particularly important to have logistic support appropriate to permit use of maximum combat power in the final stage.

Section 4. Envelopment

1. Meaning of envelopment

Weak points occurring in enemy defenses are the rear and flanks. Hence, in attacking the enemy, striking against the rear and flanks, which are the weak points, is the most effective. (See Part II, Chapter I, para. 3. b. (6), Directionality of combat power.)

Envelopment is one type of attack maneuver, containing the enemy on his front, seizing objectives in the rear of the enemy from one or both exposed flanks or possibly from the air, interdicting the enemy's route of withdrawal, and seeking to hold and destroy the enemy on the battlefield.

The envelopment, together with the turning movement, being able to strike the rear or flank which are the weak points of the enemy, has been a favorite action since ancient times.

2. Advantages of envelopment

a. It is possible to strike the flank or rear, which are the enemy's weak points.

b. The posture itself has the effects of exerting a threat to the enemy, imparting a psychology of inferiority and causing reduction or abandonment of the will to continue fighting.

c. It can interdict the enemy's line of communications and cause a drying up of the physical capability to continue fighting.

3. The enemy's countermeasures against our envelopment

Fig. 21

   a. Counterenvelopment ("an enveloping element being enveloped")

      (1) Carried out by commitment of rear-echelon units. [Fig. 21]

      (2) Accomplished by extraction and diversion of strength from another front. [Fig. 22]

Fig. 22

      (3) Retrograde movement of the entire line or a part of it, to appear on an outer flank of the enveloping unit. [Fig. 23]

 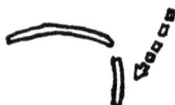 

Fig. 23       Fig. 24       Fig. 25

   b. Convex defensive formation [Fig. 24]

   c. Extending or refusing a wing [Fig. 25]

   d. Attack against the axis of envelopment [Fig. 26]

   e. Retrograde movement [Fig. 27]

Fig. 26     Fig. 27

   f. Supply and reinforcement by air

4. Conditions for success of envelopment

The conditions for success of envelopment are being able to hold and destroy the enemy on the battlefield while not giving the enemy an opportunity to take countermeasures against our envelopment action.

For this purpose, particular attention should be given to the following:

   a. Surprise attack

There must be secrecy of plans, particularly secrecy of movement of units assigned to envelopment (use of nighttime, etc.); and there must be deception, particularly dummy deployment, feints, etc., to draw the attention of the enemy to his front. In cases where tactical movement continues for two nights, secrecy of the plan is particularly important.

b.  Superiority in relative tactical mobility

In particular, use of aerial tactical mobility, equipment and maintenance of capability to overcome obstacles.

c.  Containing the enemy on his current front

In particular, securing the assault and our axis of envelopment by a determined secondary attack.

d.  Maintenance of superior combat power

In particular, the power and speed to defeat enemy counterenvelopment and other countermeasures.

e.  Concerted actions of all units

In particular, the main and secondary attacks being within supporting distance of one another.

f.  Appropriate basic disposition

In particular, it is necessary to consider this with a view toward the stage of selection of the assembly area.  However, in cases where there is a great advantage in relative tactical mobility, it is possible to overcome an unsuitable basic disposition.

5.  Relationship between strength and complete encirclement

In case of an excessive envelopment that is not in conformity with strength, even in cases of success in forming a complete encirclement, a weak point will develop somewhere, permitting the encircled force to break the encirclement or extricate itself, or causing collapse of the encirclement operation by a pincer attack accomplished by concerted action of the encircled unit with units outside the encirclement.

In the conduct of an envelopment operation, it is critically important to determine the scale of envelopment after proper evaluation of the combat power of both sides, particularly the availability of mobile combat power in the enemy's rear, and to reach the objective quickly.  If an excessive envelopment is planned with insufficient strength, even if there is success for a time in establishing complete encirclement, it is necessary to be careful subsequently about difficulty developing in maintaining it or about experiencing envelopment by the enemy and slipping into an unfavorable posture.

6.  Three-dimensional envelopment

In order to destroy the enemy through envelopment, in modern warfare, envelopment only on the ground is inadequate.  In other words, it is necessary to attempt three-dimensional envelopment by using aerial mobile power at the same time as the surface envelopment, and to interdict aerial supply and aerial reinforcement of the enemy.

Historical example: Encirclement at Sinzweya, in Burma. (Example in which Japanese forces completely encircled a British force, but the British force survived through aerial supply.)

## Section 5.  Breakthrough

1.  Essential nature of the breakthrough

The breakthrough is a type of attack maneuver that, by use of power, separates the enemy from his prepared front and seeks to lead him into piecemeal defeat or encirclement.  In other words, its essence is the application of great power, and a maximum concentration of combat power must be used.

2.  Case of effecting a breakthrough

a.  Since penetration is a tactic of power, a major prerequisite is to have overwhelmingly superior combat power or to be able to constitute it on the breakthrough front.

b.  It is carried out in cases where an envelopment or turning movement is impossible or not advantageous.

In other words, since the breakthrough is a coercive tactic against a carefully prepared enemy front, the attacker's losses also are great, and it is not a desirable measure.

Historical example:

Breakthrough of the [Japanese] 2d Division near Ang-ang-xi [Ang-ang-ch'i] in the Manchurian Incident

The German Army's breakthrough of the Maginot Line at the beginning of World War II

3.  Items for consideration in a breakthrough

a.  Use of power in the breakthrough

In order to break through and split an enemy with his resistance organized in depth, power is used successively as follows:

(1)  First, action to form a beginning for a split (formation of a breach) [Fig. 28]

It is necessary to ensure superiority of applied combat power against the breakthrough point

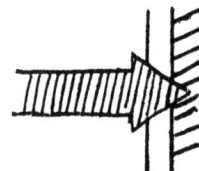

Fig. 28

(2)  Action to eliminate resistance to the break-through action (expansion of the breach) [Fig. 29]

It is necessary that the width be expanded only
to the extent that would permit deployment of
combat power able to effect a breakthrough in
depth to the objective.

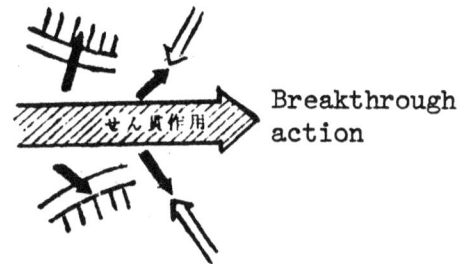

Breakthrough
action

Fig. 29

      (3)   Then, action to break through to
            the final element of the enemy
            (seizure of the final objective)
            [Fig. 30]

It is necessary not to miss the opportunity
with the combat power in depth and to apply the
breakthrough combat power until achievement of
the objective.

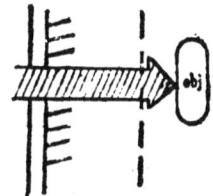

Note: 1.  Content of power in the breakthrough

      a.  Having overwhelming power

      b.  Its being maintained until achievement of the
          desired objective

Fig. 30

      c.  Application of power being swift

    2.  Countermeasures against the breakthrough

      a.  Drawing combat power from fronts other than the breakthrough
          front and reinforcing the resistance power or closing the breach

      b.  Envelopment of the breakthrough force

      c.  Abandoning resistance, withdrawing along the entire front, and
         establishing a new posture

  b.  Relationship between width and depth of the breakthrough front

The form of the breach generally is as follows:

             Trapezoid      or  Tapering in a wedge shape

Fig. 31

In other words, if the initial breakthrough-front width is large, the depth also
is great.  Hence, the necessary breakthrough front must be determined with a
view to the desired breakthrough depth.

In general, it can be said that the front width and depth of the breakthrough
are approximately equal, but the depth that can be reached in the breakthrough,

relative to the width of front, can be increased by reinforcement with tanks, artillery, and air power.

Also, at a minimum, the depth of breakthrough must be sufficient to crush the enemy's depth of organized resistance.

    c.  Selection of breakthrough point and direction

The place and direction to be penetrated makes possible the superiority of our power, and ease of application of power is the first requirement.  For this purpose, weak points of enemy disposition, terrain suitable to application of our combined combat power, etc., are selected.

Also, if other factors are disregarded, the following can be said:

    (1)  Direct breakthrough is superior to oblique breakthrough.

In case of superiority in both quality and mass, however, an oblique breakthrough also is possible.

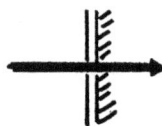 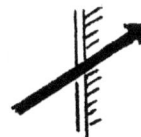

(Our power is strongest.)    (Power becomes weakened.)

Fig. 32

    (2)  Breakthrough along the direction of our line of communications [LOC] is advantageous [Fig. 33]

 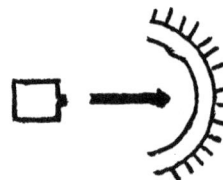

Fig. 33            Fig. 34

    (3)  Mistake of concave penetration [Fig. 34]

Enemy resistance converges [toward the center where we are attacking], and that is disadvantageous for us.

It is possible, however, if one has greatly superior firepower and tactical mobility, especially tank strength.

Historical example:  Alexander the Great's Battle of Arbela (a center breakthrough in great strength, and effective counteraction against the enemy's double envelopment).

4.  Multifront breakthroughs

    a.  Necessity of breakthroughs on several fronts

        (1)  In a one-point (one-front) breakthrough, even if success has been achieved in a tactical breakthrough with great combat power in depth, there are

many cases in which opportunity is given for the enemy to recover his strategic posture, so that, in the end, because of enemy countermeasures, this breakthrough action is not successful.

When this is considered from the viewpoint of military history:

Historical examples in World War I:

At the beginning, simple breakthroughs of prepared positions (Unsuccessful because of the defender's countermeasures)

Against limited objectives

Repeated breakthroughs (assaults)(1914 and later)

Doctrine of breakthrough by concentrated firepower (The defender also resists with power, and even tactical breakthroughs are unsuccessful)

Breakthrough in a single effort through the entire depth of the enemy force (sudden attack)(1918) (Success in tactical breakthrough, but unsuccessful because of closing of the breach by the strategic reserve)

World War II:

In the German campaign against Poland, the breakthrough of the Maginot Line, etc., there are many historical examples of success in multifront breakthroughs using armored and air power.

(2) Breakthroughs on several fronts lead easily into strategic envelopment

(a) Individual breakthroughs, in themselves, have two aims:

1 After the breakthrough, to overwhelm and destroy the enemy away from his original line of communications

2 After the breakthrough, to split, encircle, and destroy the enemy

(b) Breakthroughs on several fronts, by being combined, easily form a centripetal encirclement from several directions, and the result can be expanded to strategic scale.

(3) It is easy to split, subdivide, and destroy enemy combat power in detail.

To subdivide and destroy is a tactic of defeating in detail.

(4) In all cases, since the main objective is a decisive battle outside the positions in the enemy's rear, defeating [the enemy] is extremely sure and easy.

Strategic reserves also are brought into the encirclement and destruction

Operations of the main mobile-warfare element.

    b.   Structural characteristics of the breakthrough on several fronts

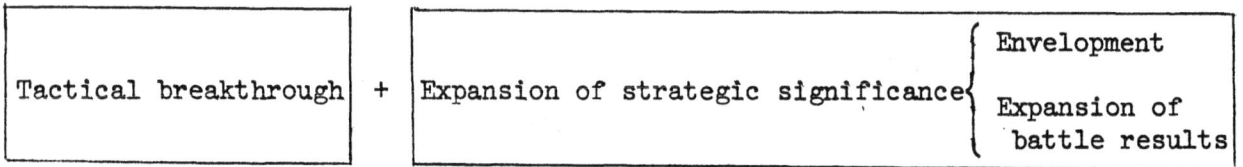

| Tactical breakthrough | + | Expansion of strategic significance | Envelopment |
| | | | Expansion of battle results |

{ Formation of breach
{ Expansion, seizure of objective

{ Envelopment, multiple envelopment
{ Divide and destroy

    (Interior-lines type) ⟶ (Exterior-lines type)

The physical structure is as shown in the figures below:

    (1)  Pincer envelopment    (2)  Multiple envelopment

Fig. 35

    (3)  Divide and destroy    (4)  Expansion of battle achievement (combined)

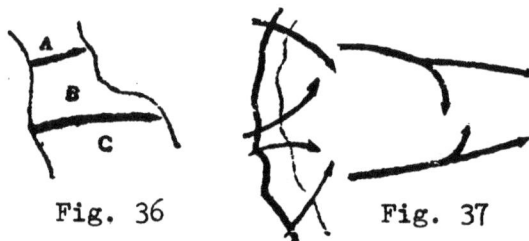

Fig. 36      Fig. 37

    c.   Tactical characteristics of the multifront breakthrough

It is basically like the characteristics of the breakthrough and is a tactic of the stronger force.

    (1)  Power, its maintenance (combat power in depth), and speed are required to a maximum degree.

This is axiomatic with respect to power plus speed = shock, but from the

- 46 -

strategic viewpoint, the necessity for combat power in depth is even greater.

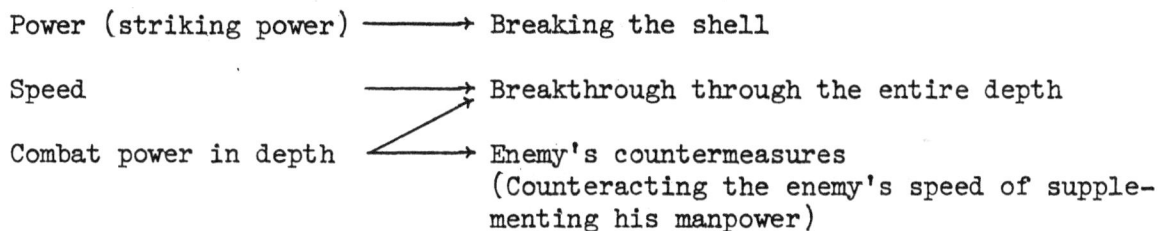

Power (striking power) ⟶ Breaking the shell

Speed ⟶ Breakthrough through the entire depth

Combat power in depth ⟵ Enemy's countermeasures
(Counteracting the enemy's speed of supplementing his manpower)

    (2) It is a combination of breakthrough and envelopment, but the breakthrough is the first impact of the operation and a measure of strategic envelopment. In other words, with the breakthrough alone, it is not possible to reach the operational objective. It is necessary to expand the tactical breakthrough into a strategic breakthrough.

    (3) It is a situation of mobile war around a breakthrough by armored combat power.

In other words, it is necessary to change the operation from stationary to movement, particularly emphasizing use of armored and air power, and it is necessary to select a breakthrough point and breakthrough direction (axis of operation) and to accomplish appropriate maneuvering.

    (4) The main objective is a decisive battle outside the position to the rear of the enemy, carried out after the breakthrough.

    (5) The surprise attack and sudden attack are emphasized.

Historical examples:

    1. Examples of success in the breakthrough on several fronts

       Breakthrough by the German Army in the Polish Campaign in World War II (pincer envelopment)

       Breakthrough of the Maginot Line by the German Army in World War II (divide and destroy)

    2. Example of failure of the breakthrough at a single point

       The offensive of the German Army in the Ardennes in the closing period of World War II

Chapter III. Eccentric Use of Combat Power

Section 1. Principle of eccentricity

1. Meaning of eccentricity

Eccentricity is the moving of the focus away from the center of a circle toward its circumference, and the principle of the application of power in cases of its repeated movement from the center of the circle toward any point on the circumference is called the principle of eccentricity.

2. Characteristics and effectiveness of eccentric action

    a. Eccentric action is the combining of power at the center and its application toward a point on the circumference.

    b. In the eccentric action, in cases of repetition of this movement, there is gradual deterioration of this nuclear power.

    c. To the extent that the power constituting the core of the eccentricity approaches the circumference, the power against the circumference increases and, conversely, it decreases toward the opposite direction.

    d. With an increase in the space of the circle, the eccentric movement becomes easier.

    e. An eccentric movement, as in the figure, is an action on interior lines and combines all power (a + b + c) against objectives one at a time.

3. Application of the principle of eccentricity

The principle of eccentricity, in regard to posture, is a passive, defensive principle of war and, in regard to combat, is applied in operations on interior lines, in defeating in detail, etc.

The enemy is on the circumference and attacks centripetally

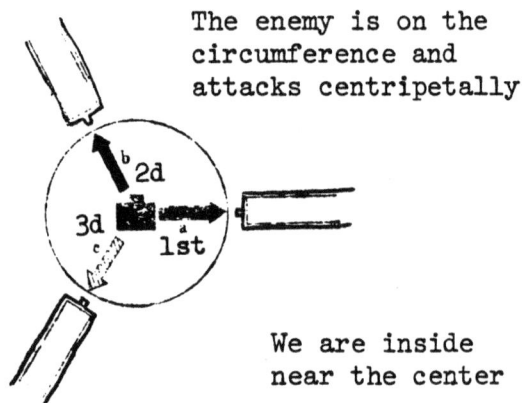

We are inside near the center

Fig. 38

Section 2.    Operations on interior lines

1. Meaning of operations on interior lines

    a. An operation on interior lines is an operation carried out with maintenance of our line of communications in the interior, directed against the enemy conducting operations centripetally toward us from several directions from the outside.

The essential of an operation on interior lines is to go against individual objectives with one's entire combined force, in other words, piecemeal defeat of an enemy split laterally or an enemy split in depth; and the concentration of combat power and the time element are of the greatest value for it.

Among recent examples, the Israeli Army's blitz campaign in the Middle Eastern war is an excellent example of operations on interior lines.

    b. Relationship between interior and exterior lines

The relationship between interior and exterior lines is a mutual relationship.

Operations on exterior lines are offensive and active, whereas operations on interior lines are defensive and passive. The relationship between the two, strategically, is naturally conditioned by the geographic relationships of the country and, in military operations, selection between interior and exterior lines can be made on the basis of the mission of the operational unit, combat power, terrain and weather conditions, etc.

Hence, conditions for occurrence of an operation on exterior lines, viewed from the opponent's side, may be said to be conditions for occurrence of an operation on interior lines. (See Part III, Chapter II, Section 2, paragraph 3.)

2.  Characteristics of the operation on interior lines

    a.  An operation on interior lines is a strategic, defensive operation.

An operation on interior lines permits a [large-unit] group of weaker combat power to assume a favorable strategic posture, seek a decisive battle, accumulate individual victories, and gain a complete victory. Hence, if one is sure of obtaining victory by power alone without the need of strategems, ordinarily operations on interior lines are not used.

    b.  It is an operation that has a great need for tactics of opportunity. There are relatively many cases in which a force operating on interior lines, to some extent, must judge its own actions on the basis of enemy moves relative to its line of communications in its interior. This involves the danger that the posture of withdrawal will be interdicted, and since it has weaknesses from the start, tactics are particularly important for the force operating on interior lines.

    c.  Changes in operations are sudden and frequent, and the tempo of the operation is rapid.

An operation on interior lines essentially is an eccentric evolution. The changes in evolution differ according to the posture of the force operating on exterior lines, increases in space, etc., but usually the speed and change of evolution are extremely large compared to those of the force operating on exterior lines.

    d.  Advantages and disadvantages of operating on interior lines

        (1)  Advantages

            (a)  Subordinate units can be combined and kept in firm control.

            (b)  Enemy elements can be defeated one after another, piecemeal.

        (2)  Disadvantages

            (a)  It is difficult to see tactical opportunities, and there is a tendency to lapse into passivity and, finally, be enveloped and compressed.

(b)  In cases where the results of piecemeal defeat are incomplete, there are subsequent difficulties.

The importance of concentrating combat power is as stated earlier, but in carrying out operations on interior lines, it is not absolutely necessary always to have units in a concentrated posture, but they can be left in a posture where they can be concentrated as desired.  On the other hand, it must be noted that there also are cases where there are disadvantages to being concentrated, such as air attack.

Historical examples:

Napoleon's Lonato operation on interior lines (1796, Italian Army against the Austrian Army)

Middle Eastern war (1967, campaign of the Israeli forces against the Arab League)

3.  Requirements for success in operations on interior lines

a.  Superiority in command and control, particularly detecting tactical opportunities, and decisive power

The operation on interior lines, since it is a posture that has weaknesses from the beginning, as stated earlier, is an action in which tactics of opportunity, skill of command, etc., exert great influence on the outcome.

Only in cases of skilful, economical use of combat power, through maintaining freedom of tactical mobility and skillfully detecting and using tactical opportunities, can the great general gain victory.

b.  Troops being elite and using mobile power well

Being in a defensive, passive posture, morale deteriorates if troops are not elite; and on the other hand, it is necessary for units to have great mobility for changing missions.

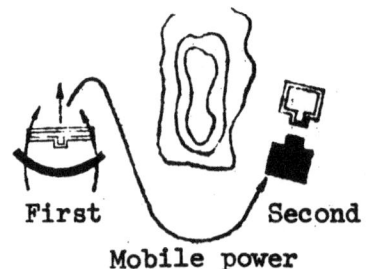

First        Second

Mobile power

Fig. 39

c.  Holding terrain for the purpose of effecting piecemeal defeat.  In other words, it is having room to maneuver.

In Figure 40, $Y^h < \dfrac{X^{km}}{V}$ (V is the speed of maneuver of B).

(1)  X is the distance that permits maintaining the terrain necessary for effecting a piecemeal defeat and is outside the limits of tactical support.  $Y^h$ is the time

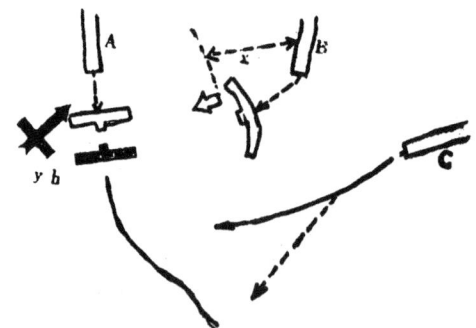

Fig. 40

- 50 -

required for the decisive battle.

(2)  In other words, during the decisive battle with enemy A, enemy B cannot approach and envelop us.  Also, it is necessary to be outside the support distance of artillery, etc., from the position of B.

(3)  X and Y are mutually related and change according to the situation. When X is close, it is necessary to have it resisted by one element.

d.  If there are defects in the physical and intangible relationships between enemy forces and in their cooperative actions, it is even more advantageous.

In modern times of advanced signal-communications measures, cooperation between forces operating on exterior lines is good, and attack by a force operating on interior lines is becoming increasingly difficult, but advantageous conditions also occur from battlefield mistakes, enemy errors, etc., and it is necessary to detect these and have countermeasures prepared to take advantage of them.

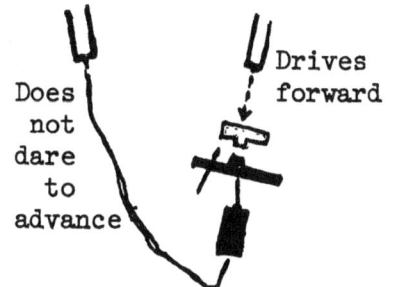

Fig. 41

e.  Having our transport in readiness

To change the employment of fighting power, quick determination and excellent implementing power are necessary; and to make this possible, it is necessary to have all types of transport in readiness and to strive to ensure tactical mobility.  At such time, in particular, a necessary condition is to secure the transport routes.

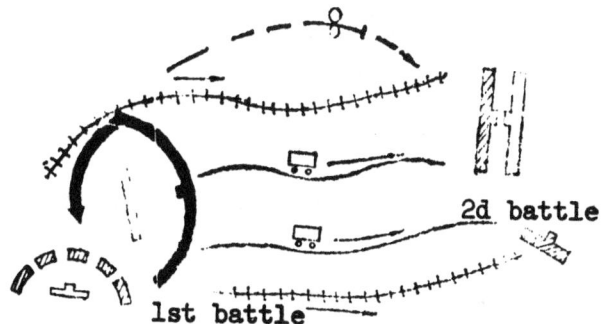

Fig. 42

f.  Existence of terrain that can disperse (split) the enemy

In order to take advantage of the enemy having split strength and to defeat him in detail, a prerequisite is to impose a posture of split strength on the enemy.

In other words, in the figure at the right, if the enemy does not advance to point A, he cannot link up (use in concert) a and b.

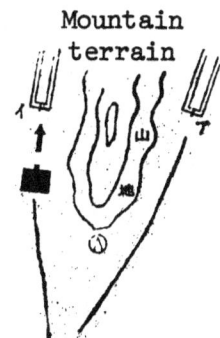

g.  Having a terrain advantage suitable for the main force defeating the enemy piecemeal while a part of the force neutralizes a portion of the enemy

(Relationship between main operation and supporting operation)

Fig. 43

Explanation has been made concerning the above operation on interior lines, but the primary objective of conducting an operation on interior lines may be said to be to ensure freedom of tactical mobility, to take advantage of splits in enemy strength, and to defeat the enemy in detail. Hence, directional orientation of the line of operations, selection of the objective, detecting opportunities to shift to other objectives, fast mobility, etc., are important major factors determining the success or failure of operations on interior lines. Also, in the conduct of operations, it is extremely important to maintain a suitable balance between the main operation (main decisive front) and supporting operations (containment fronts).

## Section 3. Defeating piecemeal

### 1. Meaning of defeating piecemeal

a. Defeating piecemeal is taking advantage of an occasion when the enemy, timewise or topographically, is separated laterally or in depth and his total combat power is not unified, and defeating one of the elements separately.

Also, the objective of defeating piecemeal is to gain local superiority over one enemy element, to defeat enemy elements separately and successively, and to gain a complete victory.

b. Defeating piecemeal, essentially, is a tactic of a weaker force and is a tactic of opportunity responding to enemy action. Hence, there is a tendency to slip into passivity and to be forestalled easily by the enemy. For this reason, to obtain its advantages, an eye for opportunity that seizes favorable opportunities is particularly important. Its greatest element is time, and herein is the principle of war.

### 2. Conditions for occurrence of defeating piecemeal

a. The enemy being in a posture of separated strength

Defeating piecemeal has as its greatest prerequisite, taking advantage of the enemy's separated strength.

(1) What is separated strength?

This is a situation in which, until completion of an operation (battle) against the enemy in one location (one enemy element), the enemy elements in other locations (other enemy elements) are separated so much from it in time or distance that they exert no direct influence.

Note: Examination in isolation of a separated condition that makes possible defeating piecemeal:

Distance of separation that is sought [is as follows:]
$X = D \times H - M$ [in which]
D = distance that can be moved in one day
H = number of days to termination of battle in the one location
M = modulus distance (conversion into distance of the time necessary for a
     reinforcing unit to deploy)

- 52 -

However, the side planning to defeat piecemeal cannot allow the opposing side the freedom to concentrate combat power. Hence, if mobility is obstructed by use of aircraft, road blocks, etc., even in cases of a short distance of strength separation, defeating piecemeal may still occur; and conversely, even if the distance is large, it does not necessarily occur. In short, other factors actually exert a greater effect than distance alone on strength separation, and is it necessary to consider the condition of strength separation in terms of the time factor more than distance.

In other words, if one refers to the sketch map in the previous section, para. 3.c., this also may be explained as

$$t = \frac{X^{km}}{V} + K > Y \text{ [in which]}$$

t = separation time

K = interdiction time (including interdiction by aviation, obstacles, or our units, enemy mistakes, etc.)

(2) Situations of definite strength separation shown in tactics

(a) Examples of lateral-separation situations

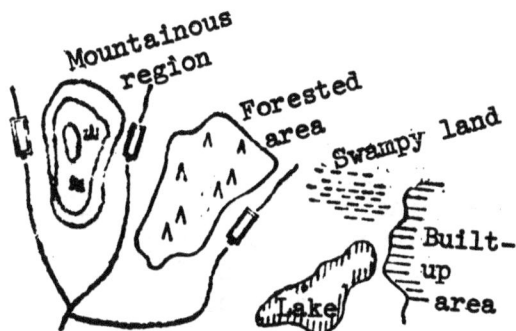

Fig. 44

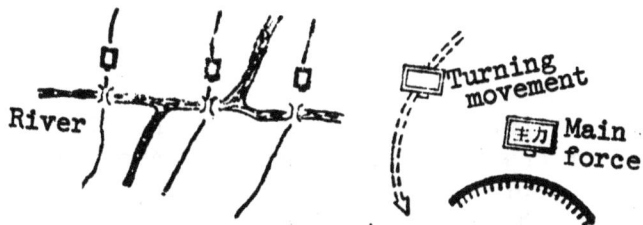

Fig. 45

(b) Examples of situations of separation in depth

c. Landing operation

d. Airborne operation (three-dimensional)

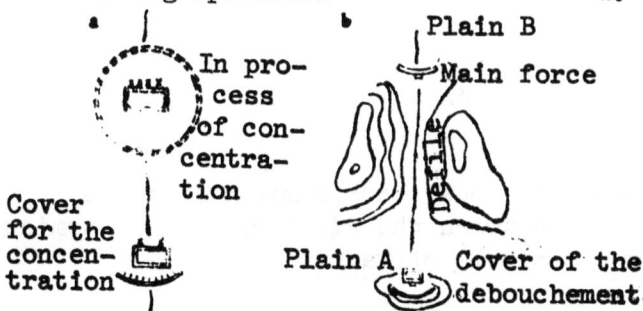

Fig. 46

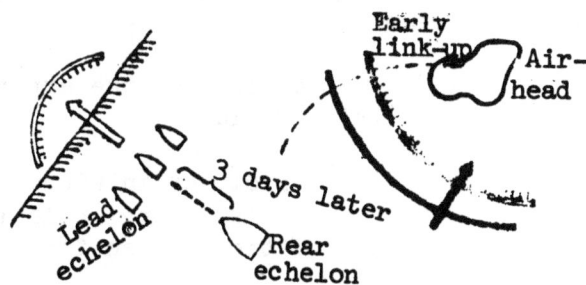

Fig. 47

- 53 -

(3)  Conditions for occurrence of situations of strength separation

If one considers cases in which a situation of strength separation occurs, one thinks of "cases of unavoidable separation" and "cases of voluntary separation."

    (a)  Cases of unavoidable separation

        <u>1</u>  Because of terrain conditions of the operational area (terrain obstacles, extent of the battlefield, degree of logistic difficulty, etc.)

        <u>2</u>  Because of weather conditions (snowfall, etc.)

        <u>3</u>  Because of obstruction by the opponent (interdiction operations, etc.)

        <u>4</u>  Other (unskillful command and control, etc.)

    (b)  Cases of voluntary separation
        Time when separation of strength is more advantageous

        <u>1</u>  When the basic disposition of combat power is dispersed. (Particularly when concentration in a single area is disadvantageous)

        <u>2</u>  When greater advantage is obtained by advancing in laterally separated elements.

        <u>3</u>  When secondary operations obtain major results.

The above classification is not necessarily a strict division.  Separation of combat power, considered from the viewpoint of the principles of war, is an error and ordinarily should be avoided.  Being in a situation where support is impossible because of distance, may be considered an exception and, in many cases, the condition is created by [enemy] action or occurs because it is fostered [by the enemy].

    b.  Piecemeal defeat occurring through taking advantage of enemy errors

Being in a posture of separated strength naturally can be considered an error; and, in final analysis, being forced, against one's will, into a posture of separated strength also must be judged a defect in command and control and in tactical capability.

    (1)  Main causes for the error of separation of strength on the battlefield

        (a)  Deficiency in signal communications, shortcomings in mutual understanding (relationship between the First and Second Armies of the Russian force in the Battle of Tannenberg)

        (b)  Unskillful tactical control (Russian Army's defense of Nanshan
             in the Russo-Japanese War)

        (c)  Forcing a posture of separation (failure of the Russian forces
             in imposing separation on the Japanese forces' First Army
             before the Battle of Mukden [1905])

    (2)  From a posture of separation

        (a) Error in strength deployment

        (b) Error in reinforcement or concentration                    Lateral separation

        (c) Error in revelation of plans                               Separation in depth

We cannot afford, however, to plan and carry out operations with an opponent's
error as a prerequisite.  If an error is discovered, it should be used effectively, and attention must be given to the paragraphs below.

    c.  Occurrence of piecemeal defeat is controlled by operational posture

A force operating on exterior lines, because of its posture, in general, cannot
defeat in detail a force operating on interior lines, but the force operating on
interior lines can easily effect a piecemeal defeat.  However, even for a force
operating on interior lines, as it is compressed into an enveloped situation,
this opportunity decreases.

The difference between an enveloped posture and a posture on interior lines is
very small.  They cannot be differentiated numerically, but if the enemy attacking from all surrounding directions can maintain tactical coordination among its
elements, there would thereafter be envelopment, and defeating [it] piecemeal
would be difficult or impossible.

    d.  Superiority must be maintainable at least on that battlefield

An inferior force that cannot maintain local superiority may be said to lack
capability.  Superiority is not limited simply to the quantity of strength, but
is a concept formed by combination of tangible and intangible elements (including items derived from morale, state of training, quality of command, posture,
etc.).  However, on the battlefield, it is difficult, in many cases, to be able
to determine this in advance.

    e.  The aggressive spirit of both sides is an important condition

Defeating piecemeal, essentially, is a tactic of the inferior force, and if it
is incomplete or fails, [that force] slips into the worst posture and, at the
best [for the opponent], could be completely annihilated.  Hence, defeating
piecemeal is easily brought about by turning the enemy's offensive spirit
against him or by fostering that.  The reason is that it is easy to organize a
battle of extermination by reverse use of shock.  (On reverse use of shock, see
Part IV.)

f.  In regard to defeating piecemeal in the second and subsequent attacks,
       it is governed by limitations on the capability of double and triple use
       of combat power and by general circumstances.

The achievement of defeats in detail in the second and subsequent attacks is
affected by the outcome of the first attack and by the general situation of both
sides.  The nature of the results of the first attack becomes a condition in the
repeated use of combat power, and at that time, the general situation must be
alleviated at least to the extent of permitting repeated use of our combat
power.  In historical examples, many cases end with the second attack.

   g.  Having superior intelligence capability that is able to learn the
       general situation of the enemy

In fact, it is important to know not only about the front where a piecemeal
defeat is being imposed, but also, regularly, about enemy developments on other
fronts.

Note:  The paragraphs below repeat explanations of the prerequisites for success
in operations on interior lines, and both should be studied together.

   h.  From the extent of separation of strength, that is, the existence of an
       area necessary for defeating piecemeal

Separation of strength, as stated earlier, is influenced greatly by other factors (physical, spiritual) added to the pure distance of separation.  In particular, it is necessary to be favored with natural geographic conditions that
cause separation of the strength of the enemy or are suitable for continuing it
for a long period of time.  On the other hand, it is necessary for these areas
to have geographic conditions suitable for our being able quickly to conclude a
decisive battle, and it is unsuitable to have terrain that is difficult for the
decisive battle, permitting tough resistance by the enemy, or that is terrain
disadvantageous to our tactical mobility.

   i.  Having air superiority and superior tactical (general) movement
       capability

In modern warfare, air superiority is an absolute condition, and even if ground
strength is inferior, defeating in detail may be achieved.

   j.  Superiority in command and control capability

For the commander, particularly the commanding general, decision-making ability
and discernment and the courage to take risky decisive action are particularly
necessary.  In the battle in East Prussia in 1914, under approximately the same
conditions, General von Prittwitz, planning to defeat in detail, abandoned his
determination in mid-course and withdrew; and on the other hand, for General
von Hindenburg, this is the good example of gaining a brilliant victory in the
Battle of Tannenberg.  Considering that defeating piecemeal is a tactic in an
extremely difficult situation, the commander must have a mental attitude to cope
with it.

Important prerequisites for achieving a defeat in detail have been discussed above, but there are extremely few situations where these conditions are complete. Hence, along with striving to create the conditions, it is necessary to carry out operations with daring determination and boldness.

Historical examples:

Napoleon's operation on interior lines in [the Battle of] Lonato

The Battle of Tannenberg and the Battle of the Masurian Lakes

Hideyoshi's Battle of Shizugatake [1583]

Operations of Japanese forces on Pacific Ocean islands

3. Cautionary items concerning carrying out the defeat in detail

    a. Selection of the objective of attack

In defeating in detail, the objective that should be attacked first is selected from those that have the following characteristics:

    (1) Enemy element that is easy to defeat

    (2) Enemy element that is most important as a threat

At that time, it is most advantageous if the element that is the objective to be defeated first is the enemy's center of gravity (pivot), that is, the enemy's main force. Also, defeating in detail differs in method according to the situation of strength separation of the enemy relative to us, and for an enemy in a situation separated in depth, in many cases, consideration of this [factor] would not be necessary.

    b. Not permitting the link-up of other enemy elements while defeating one enemy element. (Keeping pressure on the separated situation)

    (1) Making suitable selection of a battlefield

A battlefield is selected that has terrain that necessitates the desired degree of separation and blocks uniting of enemy combat power, that is easy for our tactical mobility and conduct of warfare, and that would let us carry out a quick, decisive battle while not permitting enemy link-up.

    (2) Having a suitable direction of operations (attack)

It is necessary to select a direction where enemy link-up is difficult (conversely, a direction that increases separation) or a direction where the results of the operation (attack) can directly affect the second enemy element.

Now, the direction that can obtain the greatest results, in many cases, is the direction that is most dangerous for its relation to us or to our line of communications, and for this reason, sufficient countermeasures are necessary. As in the analogy, "without entering the tiger's den, you cannot capture its cubs," obtaining major results is accompanied by risks, and in achieving a defeat in detail, it also is important to apply the principle of war of the relationship of "risk and result."

  (3) Direct obstruction of link-up with, and reinforcement of, other enemy elements

It is necessary to respond to the enemy on fronts outside the decisive battle with the minimum necessary strength and to contain superior enemy elements for a desired period of time.

 c. Acting quickly. Acting completely.

  (1) The value of the time period is decisive.

When there is insufficient rapidity in the decisive battle, that will permit coordination of forces operating on exterior lines, and defeating them in detail becomes impossible.

Also, determination, speed of positioning, and use of tactical mobility are especially important.

In regard to the use of tactical mobility, there are necessary, of course, complete tactical mobility of the force itself, and also measures to maintain freedom of movement, particularly obstruction of movement and defeat of coordination of the enemy, and preempting and securing key positions that can secure our freedom of movement, as well as holding and complete security of our axis of operations.

  (2) Boldness, decisive action from a crushing disposition of forces

When achieving defeat is incomplete, as already explained, later difficulty will occur, and this has many historical lessons, irrespective of whether it is a defeat in detail. Particularly in defeat in detail, since this has a repercussion directly affecting the entire operation, it is important to aim at complete disposition effecting decisive action enveloping or encircling the enemy on the battlefield, etc.

 d. Concentration of combat power at the decisive-battle point

In cases of defeating in detail, the characteristic of this operation may be said to be that each operation is a decisive battle and that relative combat power always is superior in each decisive battle. For this reason, one should win beginning with the first operation, in every engagement there is a decisive point, and separation and withdrawal are not permitted. Hence, decisive combat power is concentrated at each decisive point (decisive area), and combat power on the containment front is the minimum limit, without one excess, poorly stationed soldier.

e.  Perception and use of tactical opportunities and of changes in the
    situation

It is necessary to have superiority in command and control, characterized by
having use of time as its greatest value, detecting favorable opportunities for
attack against the enemy and perceiving time opportunities for change of tactics.

In particular, the extent of victory (defeating) and change in use of combat
power, change from operation on interior lines to operation on exterior lines,
etc., are extremely important.

f.  Importance of collection of intelligence information

Along with local intelligence information, intelligence information that can
explain the overall situation is particularly important throughout the entire
course of an operation.  The victory of Tannenberg, where clear-text communications were intercepted, the victory in which Napoleon near Vauchamps attacked an
enemy force that was advancing without knowing that its advance column had been
attacked and defeated, etc., are the difference of a very short period of time
in the collection of intelligence information and speak pointedly of its
importance.

Defeating in detail is a tactic of a weaker force and may be said to be a tactic
of opportunity that responds to enemy actions.  Hence, its success, in many
cases, is due to the ability of the commander, particularly of the commanding
general.  In regard to this combat, Sun Tzu, Military Strength, [Chapter] No. 5,
states, "A bird of prey's swiftly getting to break [its prey's back] is the
timing.  For this reason, a good fighter uses force fiercely and timing pre-
cisely."  ([In other words,] a skilled fighter, with strong impact force at the
moment of attack, acts with blitz action and quick reaction, giving no time for
counteraction.)  Acting in this way is considered to be the secret of defeating
in detail.  Also, modern warfare is three-dimensional warfare, it is important
not to permit combining ground and air combat power, and  one must not forget
first to defeat piecemeal with air power and to gain air superiority.

Note:  Effect of a situation of separation in depth on the selection of attack
       points

1.  The main objective in selection of attack points is to defeat in detail.

2.  Selection of a point of attack cannot be decided merely from the conditions
for defeating the enemy on that front.  The situation of the reinforcement
(rear) units also must be considered.  The main way of looking at the matter is
whether to interdict the enemy's route of withdrawal or to strike his rear.

3.  Conditions that should be considered in selecting points to be attacked

    a.  The enemy that is confronted

Military strength (large or small), strength of the position (strong or weak),
configuration of position (frontal position or flank position, etc.)

b. Reinforcement units

Military strength (large or small), time (fast or slow, amount of effect on the fighting of the confronted enemy, that is, state of separation), direction (enemy's line of communications and direction of advance)

c. Our posture

Envelopment or breakthrough; direction of line of communications

d. Terrain

Key terrain that could lead to defeating in detail

4. Examples of selection of the point of attack

a. Case where strength separation is large

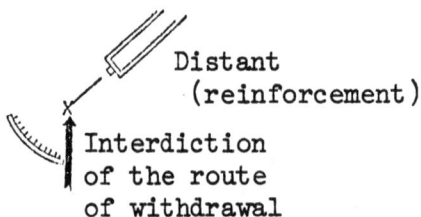

b. Case where strength separation is small

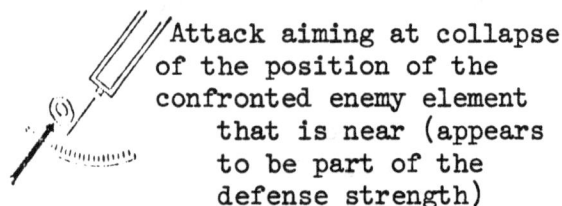

Distant (reinforcement)

Interdiction of the route of withdrawal

Fig. 48

Attack aiming at collapse of the position of the confronted enemy element that is near (appears to be part of the defense strength)

Fig. 49

Chapter IV.  Antiamphibious and Anti-Air-Landing Operations

1. Weaknesses of amphibious and air-landing operations

The greatest weakness in amphibious and air-landing operations is the time when the amphibious and air-landing units are at sea or airborne.  Next is the stage of establishment of a beachhead (airhead), when the application of organized combat power is difficult, particularly near the water's edge in amphibious operations, that is, a situation of strength separation in depth with one foot on land and one foot at sea.

However, amphibious and air-landing units regularly take countermeasures to cover these weaknesses in landings.

2. Characteristics of antiamphibious and anti-air-landing operations

a. We are passive.  (It is not known where the enemy will come.)  In other words, the enemy definitely has the initiative.

b. There are many beginnings of engagements.  (Serious consideration of beginning an engagement--it governs subsequent fortunes.)

c. There regularly are simultaneous antiamphibious or antiairborne engagements.

d.  Engagements occur suddenly, and their course is rapid.  (The balance between victory and defeat changes within a short time period.)

e.  Weaknesses of amphibious and air-landing units disappear with the passage of time.

f.  The initial engagements generally exert great influence on subsequent operations.

g.  The initial stage is a situation of divided combat power on both sides.

h.  Our air and naval strength ordinarily is inferior.

i.  Amphibious and air-landing operations are deficient in flexibility.  In other words, correcting action is ineffective.

3.  Essence of antiamphibious and anti-air-landing operations

a.  The essence of the antiamphibious and anti-air-landing operation is an offensive operation, concentrating tangible and intangible combat power prior to establishment of the enemy's beachhead (airhead) and defeating the landed enemy at an early stage.

b.  The essence of the operation in the stage of establishment of the enemy's beachhead (airhead) is to destabilize the combat situation, concentrate decisive combat power, and strike.  At that time, resolute defense of key positions on the battlefield is particularly important.

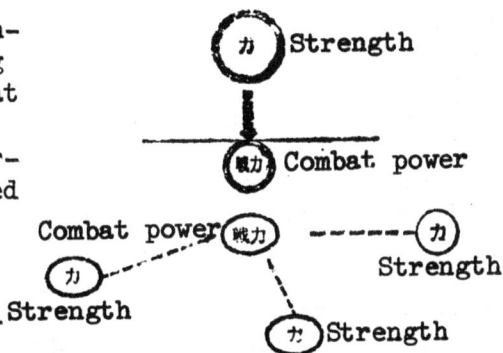

First stage

Fig. 50

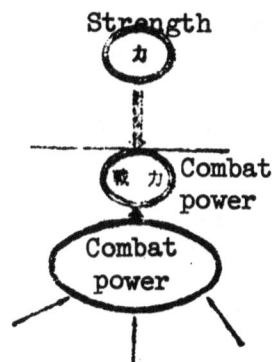

Second stage

Fig. 51

c.  In summary of the above, the essence of antiamphibious and anti-air-landing operations, in the end, is a race to concentrate combat power at landing points, and victory in this wins victory in the antiamphibious and anti-air-landing operations.

Historical examples:

Examples of success in amphibious operations:

The Normandy landing operation of the Allied forces

Various operations of U.S. forces on Pacific islands (Saipan, Guam, Iwo Jima, Okinawa, etc.)

The Malay landing operation of the Japanese forces

Example of failure in an amphibious operation:

The Gallipoli landing operation

Part IV.  TURNING AN ENEMY'S COMBAT POWER AGAINST HIMSELF

Chapter I.  Reverse Use and Manipulation of Momentum

1.  Meaning of reverse use of momentum

a.  Momentum

The term momentum, as used here, means the power of the enemy's offensive drive against us.  In other words, it indicates the will and power and action of the offensive drive.

b.  Reverse use of momentum

Reverse use of momentum is a principle of war that uses an enemy's momentum in reverse, seeking to seize superiority in use of relative combat power, and it has a thread of connection with the judo secret of "using the opponent's strength, applying our trick, and throwing the opponent."

c.  Characteristics of reverse use of momentum

(1)  If this principle of war is applied skillfully, the enemy can be forced into a decisive battle, or the opportunity can be grasped for a battle of extermination.

Also, to some extent, the greater the enemy's momentum, the greater the success will be, and a small force can well deliver a crushing blow to a large enemy force.

(2)  In other words, initially, the enemy is caused to apply this momentum fully, and since, with our resistance, the enemy's momentum decreases during the course of the engagement and we gain superiority in posture, in the end, we gain superiority in relative combat power and attempt to defeat (destroy) the enemy.

(3)  When the enemy's momentum is taken from the enemy, it is greater for us if the terrain includes a lure.

A lure is constituted in cases where the enemy is judged superior in relative posture and in combat power and able to destroy or defeat us, or in cases where there is a key terrain position that controls the battlefield or definitely should be secured for the conduct of military operations.

2.  Decoying, entrapping

a.  Meaning of decoying and entrapping

Decoying and entrapping mean the management of enemy momentum with the aim of achieving superiority in relative combat power. In other words, it is to lure the enemy force into a place or direction that we desire (or have planned in advance) with the objective of creating a situation where defeat (destruction) of the enemy is possible (for example, a situation where, in view of posture and terrain, applying our combat power is easy and applying enemy combat power is difficult).

Also, in order to decoy and entrap, it is necessary to present the enemy with a lure. Among these lures are key terrain, dummy units, resources, etc.

    b. Application of decoying and entrapping

The principle of war of decoying and entrapping can be applied in all localities of military operations (battles), but examples of its typical uses are as follows:

      (1) Battle of extermination

      (2) Decoying the enemy in order to shift to the offensive

      (3) Mobile defense

      (4) Ambush-attack tactic

      (5) Antitank pocket

      (6) Antiairborne pocket

      (7) Pocket of fire

Also, it is important to note that a reentrant position is not used with decoying and entrapping. The reason is that the attacker, avoiding the error of the reentrant penetration, necessarily attacks from one flank.

    c. Cautionary items in decoying and entrapping

      (1) It is desirable that the direction of decoying or entrapping coincide with the enemy's main approach route.

      (2) The size of the area into which the enemy is decoyed or entrapped is such that the enemy force that enters it is appropriate for our striking power.

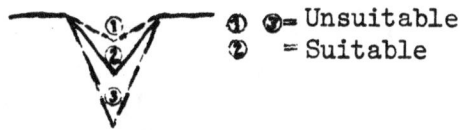

Good     Bad     Bad

Fig. 52

      (3) Consideration of the relationship between the size of the area into which the enemy is decoyed or entrapped (troop strength decoyed or entrapped) and the frontage [Fig. 53]

① ③ = Unsuitable
② = Suitable

Fig. 53

(4)  In regard to determining the area into which to decoy or entrap, consideration of terrain and our direction of strike, etc., after the decoying or entrapping.

(5)  In regard to planning the decoying or entrapping, the following items are considered:

        (a)  Full consideration of the character and usual tactics, etc., of the enemy force.

        (b)  Avoiding excessively unnatural decoying and entrapping.  (Our plans are easy for the enemy to detect.)

        (c)  Having countermeasures prepared in case planned decoying or entrapping cannot be accomplished.

Since the enemy also has free will, it is absolutely necessary to take into consideration his not acting in accordance with our desires.

Historical examples:

    Battle of Austerlitz (Battle of the Three Emperors)(1805, Napoleon against the allied Russian and Austrian armies)(example of decoying and entrapping)

    See historical examples of extermination [Part IV, Chapter III]

## Chapter II.  Diversion and Countered Diversion

### Section 1.  Meaning and characteristics of diversion and countered diversion

1.  Diversion

Diversion means drawing as many enemy elements as possible away from the desired area for our main force or preventing the enemy's freedom of action, with the objective of dispersing and reducing enemy combat power used in our main force's area and giving us the advantage in relative combat power in the main force's area.

2.  Threat

    a.  Threat means threatening with force (with or without action) in order to cause the enemy to feel distress and to create a sensation of psychological disadvantage.

Threat is psychological.  Since the sensation of psychological effect increases with increases in the extent that the opponent fears us, in cases where the opponent is excessively nervous or has memories of trying experiences, it is further increased.  Hence, it can be said that, for the defeated, the enemy threat is great.

The effect of threat decreases in cases of "it is secure," "it is safe," etc.

b. Receptivity to threats

Since threat has the objective of psychological effect (causing a sensation of psychological disadvantage), the enemy's receptivity to threats is not simply an intangible problem, but differs according to the character of the enemy force, the place where the threat is imposed, opportunities, the degree of enemy preparation, the threatening force, etc.

In other words,

(1) Enemy's character

A nervous enemy, an enemy that has a feeling of fear of us > [= is greater (in receptivity) than] an enemy with great self-confidence from a great deal of combat experience.

(2) Place (area)

Front < [= is less than] flank < rear

(3) Opportunity

Opportunities that can be forecast < sudden, unexpected opportunities that exert great, general effect.

(4) Degree of preparation

Being prepared < being unprepared

Countering troop units and measures < noncountering troop units and measures

(5) Threat power

Diversion element having combat power that is small < combat power that is large.

3. Relation between diversion and threat

Diversion is manifested as a result of a threat. In other words, if a threat is effective, it causes the enemy to formulate some countermeasures, and threat and diversion being mutually related, if a threat is successful, its result is a diversion.

Also, the threat is an action, and the diversion indicates the commander's plan or objective.

Note: Containing means to hold the enemy and not permit freedom of action. In other words, it means a condition in which the effectiveness of a diversion is continued. Holding means to keep the enemy grasped or to limit or stop the enemy's freedom of action.

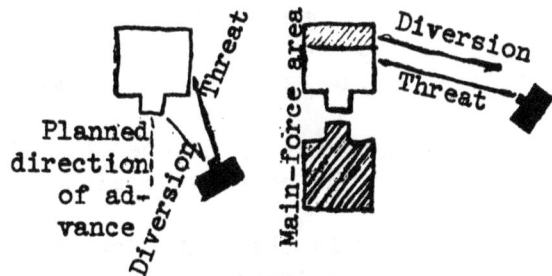

Fig. 54

- 65 -

4. Measures and methods of the diversion

As stated above, for the diversion, it is necessary to present a major threat to the enemy, and for this purpose, there are the following measures and methods:

    a.  Method through attacking

        (1)  A determined attack has great receptivity for the threat it presents to the enemy, and it is the best method for a diversion.

        (2)  An attack against a prepared enemy front has little threat effectiveness.  In this case, it must have sufficient power to cause failure of the enemy's battle line.

        (3)  In cases of diversion by an attack, sufficient consideration must be given to the following items:

            (a)  Time of attack

            (b)  Part of the tactical formation against which the attack is delivered

            (c)  Power (violence) of the attack

            (d)  Method of carrying out the attack

In other words, it is necessary to carry out a sudden, powerful (violent) attack at a time and place that causes most distress to the enemy and is as far as possible away from our main force.

Historical examples:

    Attack from the eastern wing of the Yalu Army in the Battle of Mukden [1905]

    Operation of Wingate's Special Force before the Imphal Campaign

    b.  Method through the existence method (method of being located at a given point and presenting a glaring threat)

In cases where it appears at a place that is distressful to the enemy, if the enemy leaves it alone, there are major results, and even without direct attack, the enemy can be diverted and held.  However, since the enemy has sufficient time to take countermeasures, this method generally has little effectiveness.

        (1)  Restriction of operational objective (direction) by the relative positions of both sides

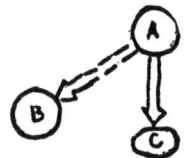

Fig. 55

        (a)  In the figure at the right, A has B as its natural tactical objective, but since C is in a position where it restricts that action, it is a case where some countermeasure first must be taken against C.  A good example of this is the relationship of the Russian Army (A) with the German Army (B) and Austrian Army (C) at the beginning of World War I.

      (b)  The figure at the right is the case of occupying a position to the flank of the enemy's line of operations and forcing the enemy to change his line of operations and his operational front.

Fig. 56

    (2)  Case of restricting the action of a unit

      (a)  By the existence of airmobile units (airborne units, heliborne units, etc.), a constant threat is presented to the rear area, freedom of movement of the opposing units is limited, and they are held in the rear area.

      (b)  An opposing force is held in its area by means of the existence of a ranger (guerrilla) unit.  A good example was in the Korean War, where one-third of the force had to be assigned to rear-area security to act against guerrilla bands of the Communist forces.

  c.  Method through defense

Since diversion through defense arises in conjunction with enemy offensive action, it is not possible to achieve a diversion at the time we desire.  Also, diversion through defense is dependent upon self-confidence relative to the defense (strength of defense, strength of organization of firepower, etc.).

In cases where, if there is enemy offensive action, this is turned against the enemy, and we withdraw power [for use elsewhere] and, by defense against the superior enemy with inferior strength, can achieve diversion and a holding action.  Hence, in cases of seeking diversion through defense, it is necessary to present a lure to the enemy and  draw the enemy's offensive.

5.  Effectiveness of diversion and its continuance

  a.  **Effectiveness of diversion**

    (1)  Proof of diversion success    (2)  Proof of diversion failure

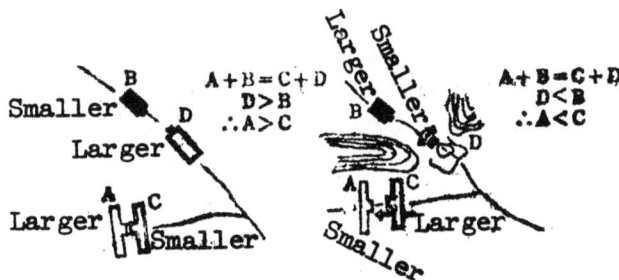

Fig. 57

  b.  Continuance of effectiveness of diversion

Diversion, in cases where its method of accomplishment is suitable, can achieve suitable effectiveness at the beginning, but with the passage of time, the situation is perceived by the enemy, the enemy causes a countered diversion and takes countermeasures, and the effectiveness of the diversion is lost.

Since the effectiveness of diversion depends on interaction with the enemy's alertness, the character of the enemy general, etc., it generally is a completely unknown quantity, and estimating the probability of success is difficult. Hence, it is necessary to be fully aware that there are limitations to success.

6. Countered diversion

Countered diversion means a situation in which the unit assigned to the diversion is checked by a weaker part of the enemy force while the enemy concentrates his combat power in another area.

For the element effecting a diversion, there is always the possibility of a countered diversion.

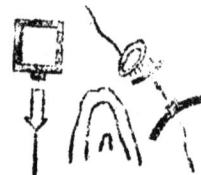

Example 1: Case of being checked by a weaker element of the enemy, while the main force of the enemy maintains its freedom of action. [Fig. 58]

Fig. 58

Example 2: Shift from defense to countered diversion

(1) Diversionary attack by the enemy

Attempt at diversion of our
    general reserve

Decisive battle

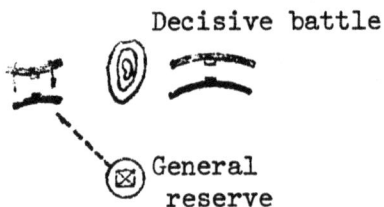

General
reserve

Fig. 59

From defense to
countered di-
version. One
element remains

Elements in-
crease the
main force,
joining in the
decisive battle

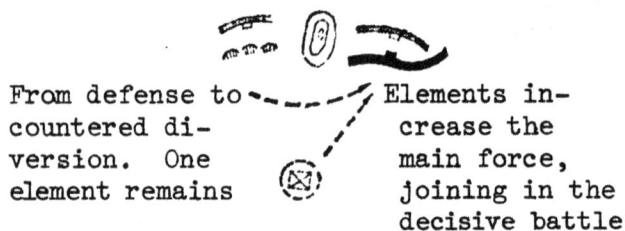

Fig. 60

7. Characteristics of a diversionary operation

   a. It is a secondary operation of a main operation.

   b. The opposing enemy is greatly superior.

   c. It is restricted in time and space by the main operation.

   d. In general, it is deceptive in nature.

   e. Basically a decisive battle should be avoided, but in some circumstances, a decisive battle is advantageous or necessary.

Section 2. Relationship between the main operation and secondary operation

1. Meaning of main operation and secondary operation

A main operation is an operation that orients the main effort of the unit engaged in the operation, that is, an operation that seeks to achieve the main objective of the operation. The secondary operation is an operation in an area separated from the main operation, for the purpose of facilitating the main operation, that is, it is an operation that seeks to achieve the secondary objective of the operation. Also, the front that is carrying out the main operation is called the main-operation front, and the front that is carrying out the secondary operation is called the secondary-operation front.

2. Relationship between the main operation and the secondary operation

a. There also are cases where a force has sufficiently great combat power to be able to take the offensive on two fronts at the same time, but, in general, a decisive battle is sought first on the main-operation front, and following that, strength is diverted to the secondary-operation front and a decisive battle occurs there. Hence, in such a case, ordinarily, during the initial period, a "delaying operation" is carried out in the secondary operation.

b. Victory in the two-front operation (an operation carried out simultaneously on two fronts that are strategically separated) is determined by the result of the decisive battle on the main-operation front in the initial period. However, the operation on the secondary-operation front exerts a large influence on the operation on the main-operation front and also governs the general outcome of the operation.

c. Until completion of the decisive battle on the main-operation front, the secondary-operation front necessarily is limited to the minimum necessary combat power and, in many cases, conduct of that operation is under extremely difficult conditions.

d. When the secondary operation fails, of course, even though the operation itself is evolving advantageously, to the extent that it exerts a bad effect on the main operation, there is a failure from the viewpoint of the overall operation.

e. The secondary operation, in order to facilitate the main operation, must simply take the offensive with the secondary objectives of the main operation of "repulse of the enemy in the given area," "possession of the given area," "threat," etc. (The offensive operations of the Yalu River Army in the Russo-Japanese War were of this type.)

3. Characteristics of the secondary operation

a. It is a subsidiary operation of the main operation.

b. It is limited in time and space by the main operation.

c.  It is an operation limited in combat power and in all other conditions.

d.  The opposing enemy is greatly superior.

### Section 3.  Delaying operation

1.  Meaning and objective of the delaying operation

The delaying operation is an operation subsidiary to the decisive battle, and it is an operation which, in order to make the overall operation advantageous and easy, is conducted with the objectives of avoiding decisive battle and using combat power economically, forcing casualties from the enemy, and obtaining a margin of time or diverting and containing the enemy, etc.

Hence, this type of operation is carried out:

As an operation on a secondary-operation front subsidiary to the main operation (lateral relationship),

During the interval until the shift to a decisive battle on the main-operation battlefield (relationship in depth).

For example, the former is "the eastern operations of the German Army in the initial part of World War I" and the latter is "operations in the Korean War until the Pusan Beachhead."

2.  Characteristics of the delaying operation

a.  Since this operation is a subsidiary operation, it is restricted in time and space by the planning and actions of the decisive-battle force (main force), and the operation must be conducted under certain requirements.

b.  This operation, in general, is an operation by an inferior force against a superior force.

c.  This operation, sooner or later, is changed to a different tactical objective.  Delaying-objective A is changed to delaying-objective B and finally is changed also to decisive combat.

d.  In this operation, the combat power of the force conducting the operation undergoes many changes, for example, strength being withdrawn to be given to another force or the reverse, receiving strength from another force.

e.  This operation initially should avoid decisive combat and try to preserve combat power, but, depending on the situation, there also are cases where, as an expedient, a decisive engagement is daringly effected.

In summary, a delaying operation is an operation under extremely difficult conditions, the measures and methods for carrying out the operation are varied and have no definite rules, and it must be conducted as a flexible engagement that displays all sorts of cleverness.

Also, the conduct of this operation requires judging appropriately the contradictions of thinking that seeks to fulfill the requirement of avoiding defeat through secure positioning and the necessity of taking hazardous decisive action when opportunities are seen. This is the reason that this operation is said to be difficult. Hence, it should be borne in mind that, if the delaying operation is not assigned a greatly superior commander and staff with a very well trained unit, achievement of the objectives of this operation will be difficult.

3. Measures and methods of the delaying operation

The delaying operation, in character, has great variety of condition, and its measures and methods cannot be judged by definite rules, but usually, one first considers the time that the delay should last and the terrain that should be used in accordance with the mission and the situation of both sides (particularly the relationship between the enemy's situation and the decisive engagement), then determines the "suicide site" position for the final decisive engagement, and with these as bases, determines the general course of the subsequent conduct of the operation.

Measures are offensive, defensive and combinations of those, but most cases decide upon the defensive.

    a. Offensive

        (1) In the delaying operation, the force conducting the operation must particularly maintain its freedom of operation, and the best method of doing this is the offensive. However, it must not, by rushing rashly, dissipate combat power too rapidly, and lose operational freedom. Especially in cases of a delaying operation with a large unit, it is planned to achieve the objective by the offensive, insofar as the situation permits.

        (2) Attack (decisive strategic engagement)

In cases of a definite chance of victory or where achievement of minimum mission is not possible without an attack, an attack must be made resolutely. Of course, the attack is easy to conduct, and if it is successful, great combat success can be achieved, but dissipation of combat power also is rapid, and if it should end in defeat, operational freedom is lost. Hence, particular consideration is necessary concerning undertaking an attack.

Items that should be considered for an attack are as follows:

        (a) Consideration of achieving a minimum mission, even if the attack fails.

        (b) Giving particular attention to selection of the place for the attack.

        (c) Making advantageous an attack with a limited objective.

        (d) In many cases an interception tactic is advantageous.

(e) There also are cases where it is advantageous to make attacks successively on various parts of the battle line in a systematically planned sequence.

(f) There also are cases where attack is advantageous in conjunction with delaying action and other diversionary attacks.

(g) Besides, there are the limited attack and the decoy attack.

b. Defensive

From the essential character of the delaying operation, an attack that risks the fate of our force, except in special cases, cannot be called appropriate. Hence, most cases are based on defensive methods.

Defensive methods include the following:

Defense (securing a definite area)

Delaying action

Using both in combination

However, since the defensive operation has the defect of easily exerting a bad psychological effect on the unit, this point requires particular attention.

(1) Defense

Defense is the strongest measure among the defensive actions, and use of this method for holding an area is a good plan, but we also have a danger from the essential nature and objective of the delaying operation, which is not very different from the attack in dissipation of combat power. In defense, if the enemy's strength decreases and he holds his position, it becomes a confrontation. In confrontation, interdiction and blocking of the [enemy's] line of communications are necessary.

(2) Delaying action

This action is a continuous operation that makes combined use of resistance and withdrawal, and since it naturally is easy to come to employ the unit passively, it is particularly necessary to maintain the unity and coordination of actions of all front-line units in order to preserve the discipline and freedom of the operation.

Also, characteristics of this operation are disruption of organizational unity, wavering and intermingling of units, decline in morale, attrition of strength, etc.

Historical examples:

Operations of the Allied forces in the Korean Campaign until the Pusan beachhead

- 72 -

Operation "Dan," Phase 2 and Phase 3, carried out by the [Japanese] Thirty-third Army in Northern Burma [1944]

c.  Other

The items listed below are much used in strategic delaying and also are necessary in tactical delaying

(1)  Delaying by use of fortifications

It is organized laterally and in depth and there also are cases with use of islands.  (Examples:  Maginot Line, Siegfried Line)

(2)  Delaying based on ranger warfare

(3)  Propaganda strategy

(4)  Air assault

Section 4.  Unit acting on the flank of the main force

1.  Summary

In this section are discussed the operations of a unit that has the main mission of diversion and containment and that acts on the flank of the main force.  This unit, in its time and space relationship to the main force, must give maximum consideration to whether it can somehow contribute to the operations of the main force.

In other words, it is the principle of war that "[if the main confrontation is] close, [the flank unit must operate] close," "[if the main confrontation is] distant, [the flank unit must operate] distant."

2.  Form of threat

a.  The enemy first defeats our threatening unit in detail

b.  The enemy, enduring temporary distress, is intent on a decisive engagement

c.  The enemy, with one part of his force, copes with our threatening unit

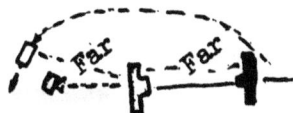

d.  The enemy experiences great distress

Fig. 61

- 73 -

Consideration of the form of threat is as in the above figure. Based upon this, a discussion of the desirable time for a diversion and relative positions of both sides is given below.

3.  Time relationship (time of diversion)

   a.  The time when a unit with the mission of diversion imposes a threat must yield an effect that directly benefits the action of the main force or is usable by that force.

   b.  In cases where the timing of diversion is unsuitable, the diversion is ineffective and troops become poorly dispositioned or are defeated in detail.

For example, in the figure at the right, in cases where there is still a margin of time in the decisive engagement in the main-force area, if unit C, assigned to diversion, advances close to B, B would first defeat C in detail and then strike A.

[Unit] A cannot yet use these results. Hence, C must be placed where it is not defeated in detail and it must act in concert with A and engage in an action that is effective at the time of A's decisive engagement.

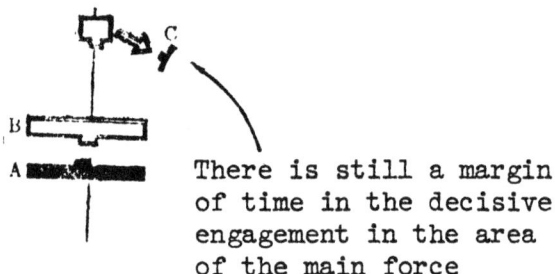

There is still a margin of time in the decisive engagement in the area of the main force

Figure 62

Historical example:  The Russian Army's "Mishchenko cavalry group's operations near the sea district" in the Russo-Japanese War (example of error in the timing of a diversion).

4.  Space relationship (relative positions of the two sides)

   Example 1:  Case where the main forces of both sides are far apart

   a.  In cases like that of the figure at the right, B, after defeating C or managing in such a way as to make a first strike impossible, moves against A.  The effort of C may be great, but the diversion is ineffective.

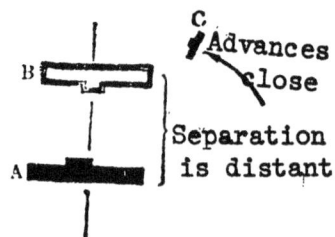

Fig. 63

   b.  In cases like that of the figure at the right, if B tries to deal with C, action of A becomes easy, and if it tries to deal with A, C becomes distressed and the diversion is ineffective.

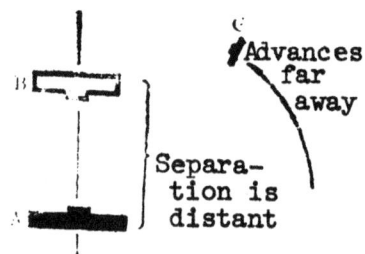

Fig. 64

- 74 -

Example 2:   Case where the main forces of both sides
             are close together

a.   In cases like that of the figure at the right,
B is threatened in front by A and in the rear by C, and
dealing with them is extremely difficult.  If an attempt
is made to deal with one of them, the other takes advantage of the situation, and if it deals with both, its
strength is divided, and the effect [of the diversion]
is great.

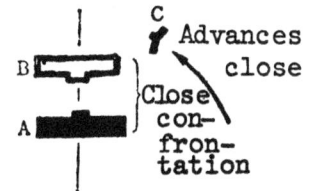

Fig. 65

b.   In cases like that of the figure at the right,
even though B sustains a threat temporarily from C,
it first defeats A and then has the capability to
move against C.  However, at this time, there also
are cases of effective diversion by advancing to key
terrain on the enemy's route of withdrawal.

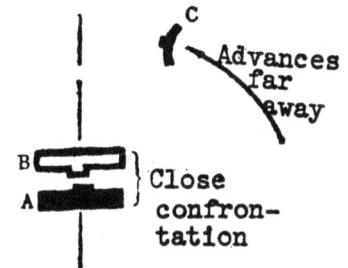

Fig. 66

5.   Relationship between the decisive engagement of
     the main force and units operating on its flank

What is suitable as principles of war for units operat-
ing on the flank of the main force must be judged in the light of the timing and
spatial (relative position) relationship to the main force.  In other words, it
is essential to be careful not to be defeated piecemeal, to contribute to the
decisive engagement of the main force, and not to become poorly dispositioned
remote from the action.

Examples may be shown as follows:

| Time of decisive engagement of the main force | Action of extreme flank unit |
|---|---|
| Case of existence of relative margin (for example, 10 days or longer) | It secures subsequent freedom of action and advances into a suitable flank position where it cannot be defeated in detail |
| Case of no margin (for example, 2-3 days) | Advance to the enemy's rear (march distance of 2-3 days) or to near the flank or rear of the enemy |

| Beginning of decisive engagement | Immediately thereafter (uncertainty of the outcome) | Mounting a diversionary attack against the enemy's flank or rear |
|---|---|---|
| | Favorable case | Advance to the enemy's flank or rear (key position on the route of withdrawal) |
| | Unfavorable case | Attacking the enemy's flank or rear |

Chapter III.  The Battle of Extermination on the Battlefield

1.  Meaning and characteristics of the battle of extermination

a.  The battle of extermination has the ideal of annihilating and leaving no survivors; but, from ancient times, examples of such battles of extermination are relatively rare.  Hence, one in which more than half of the enemy force is destroyed or captured is called a battle of extermination.

b.  Characteristics of the battle of extermination

(1)  Fortuitousness of the battle of extermination

The battle of extermination is related not only to our doing our utmost to achieve it but also to the nature of the enemy's actions, so that if the enemy does not have a determined will to fight, it occurs relatively rarely.  In other words, when the conditions for occurrence of a battle of extermination listed below are met, it occurs, but there is no disputing the fact that it includes a large element of good luck.

(2)  Riskiness of the battle of extermination

The normal form of the battle of extermination is annihilation of a weaker force with a strong will to fight, by an overwhelmingly stronger force, but it is always difficult to anticipate this.

In cases of acting with a force that is equal to, or weaker than, the enemy, fighting safely and comfortably by avoiding a position of defeat throughout the entire operation, it is too much to hope to annihilate the enemy.  The principal requirements for occurrence of annihilation, all are unfavorable or dangerous for us.  One must expect to confront very many unforeseen, dangerous situations when carrying out a complete envelopment, turning movement, rear attack, interdiction of the route of withdrawal, etc., which are inherently necessary in implementation of a battle of extermination.

2.  Conditions for occurrence of a battle of extermination

a.  It is both opposing forces planning a decisive engagement, or the enemy advancing with fierce momentum.  With the battle of extermination, naturally, the probability [of occurrence] is greater, the greater the superiority of one side in combat power, and this is the reason that there are many historical examples of an inferior force annihilating a superior force.

The battle of extermination usually is difficult against an enemy that is carrying out a delaying operation.

b.  One of the forces having a deterioration in morale and, with the final period of its offensive or the extension of its line of operations, experiencing a decline in combat power, the other force then being in a position where it can force the former into a decisive engagement.

c.  Superiority in firepower and interdiction of the route of withdrawal being possible at the decisive point.

    d.  There being superiority in command and control, particularly a great difference in the command abilities of both force commanders.

    e.  A unit being exceptionally strong, and its quality being greatly superior to that of the enemy.

    f.  There being many possibilities for surprise attack, in particular, there being superiority in concealing plans and in using tactical mobility.

3.  Relation between risk and success

    a.  In order to obtain great success, great risk is necessary.

In order to obtain great success such as a battle of extermination, it is necessary that the enemy's momentum be large, and on that front, we must accept the possibility of slipping into an extremely dangerous situation.  In other words, a great risk must be accepted.

    b.  In history, there are more examples of overcoming risks and obtaining a great victory than of being defeated because of hazardous action.  However, there must be sufficient countermeasures against the risk.

"Great success lies in fearlessly taking risks, but before action, careful consideration is necessary" (the great Moltke).

    c.  In regard to taking a risk, the degree of risk to accept is determined simply by the characteristics of the enemy, the capability of our force, confidence in our commanding, etc.  In other words, appropriately judging the degree of risk must be made with a knowledge of the enemy and knowledge of oneself.  For that reason, it is necessary to consider the relationship between risk and results in the comparison of our courses of action (paragraph 4) in the [commander's] estimate of the situation.

Historical examples:

    The envelopment annihilation Battle of Cannae (216 [B.C.], Roman army against Hannibal's army)

    The annihilation Battle of Tannenberg (1914, German army against the Russian army)

    Battle of the Masurian Lakes (1915, German army against the Russian army)

    Battle of Caporetto (1917, German and Austrian armies against the Italian army)

    Besides the above, the suicidally heroic battles of La-meng [Yunnan], Teng-yue [T'êng-yüeh (=Teng-chong, Yunnan, 1944)], Saipan, Attu, etc., strictly speaking, also are battles of extermination.

# Part V. HOLDING THE INITIATIVE

## Chapter I. Summary

### 1. Holding the initiative

Holding the initiative is acting independently and aggressively with a fine planning sense, imposing our will, and gaining a position that dominates the combat situation.

Hence, holding the initiative is extremely important for reaching the objective of the operation (gaining the victory).

### 2. Conditions for ensuring holding the initiative

#### a. Seizing the initiative

The first condition is to determine our will independently and establish a plan quickly before the enemy does his, in order to seize the initiative and conduct an active operation that holds the initiative.

For this reason, it is particularly important, by reading the mind of the enemy general and by foreseeing and discerning wisdom and careful preparation, to take the enemy by surprise and seize the initiative.

Also, holding the initiative is related to tactical mobility, and it is necessary, by quick tactical movement, excellent planning sense, and ingenuity, always to hold the initiative.

#### b. Gaining a position to control the combat situation

In order to gain a position to control the combat situation, it is particularly important to preempt key positions that control the combat situation. For this purpose, it is necessary to obtain reliable intelligence information before the enemy does, make thoroughgoing preparations, and apply superior combat power to key positions that control the combat situation.

### 3. Holding the initiative in all tactical actions

a. Attack (attack on a position)--initiative is with us.

b. Defense--initially, the initiative is not with us but with the enemy.

c. Meeting engagement--there are various types of cases, the initiative being with us or with the enemy.

## Chapter II. The Meeting Engagement

### 1. Condition of occurrence of the meeting engagement

As conditions for occurrence of the meeting engagement, the following are considered:

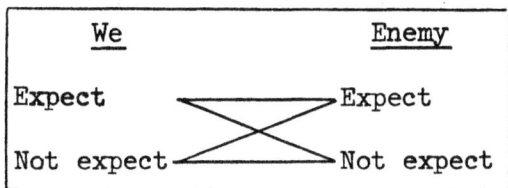

| We | | Enemy |
|---|---|---|
| Expect | | Expect |
| Not expect | | Not expect |

Fig. 67

There are four types of conditions, as in the figure at the left, the most desirable one being with us expecting and the enemy taken by surprise.
(Retention of the initiative)

## 2. Securing the initiative in a meeting engagement

The essence of the meeting engagement is to gain the initiative by placing the enemy in a passive posture.

For this reason, items which should receive particular care are as follows:

| | Initially | Thereafter |
|---|---|---|
| We | Initiative | Initiative |
| Enemy | Initiative | Passive |

Fig. 68

a. Preemption (securing) of key positions

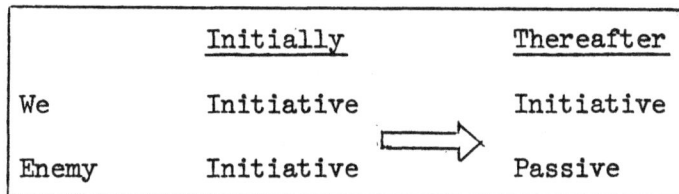

Key positions that control the combat situation are occupied before the enemy, and the initiative on the battlefield is secured.

b. Rapid deployment to a favorable posture

By using rapid tactical mobility, we deploy rapidly into a favorable posture before the enemy achieves it. At that time, it is necessary to make an all-out effort to mount an enveloping attack against the enemy.

c. Organization of combat power

In the meeting engagement, in order to concentrate superior combat power at the decisive point and overcome the enemy, it is necessary quickly to coordinate and organize combat power, especially artillery firepower. It must be remembered that tactical movement unaccompanied by firepower is not effective.

## 3. Piecemeal commitment to battle or coordinated attack

The decision on piecemeal commitment to battle or a coordinated attack is made principally on the basis of which side secures key positions that control the combat situation.

In other words, in cases where the enemy secures the key positions, the coordinated attack is usual; and in cases where we control the key positions, in order to expand that success rapidly, piecemeal commitment to combat is usual.

4.  **Essentials of deployment in an oblique meeting engagement**

    a.  **Types, and advantages and disadvantages**

        (1)  Inner-flank deployment

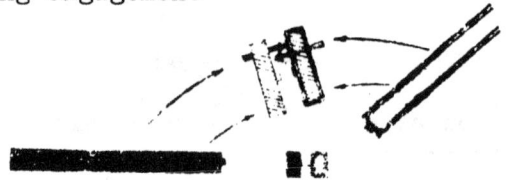

Fig. 69

Rapid deployment holds and increases the gains of the advance guard, and in favorable cases, has the advantage of being able to attack the enemy's flank.  When the speed of deployment of both sides is the same, there necessarily also develops a frontal attack.

        (2)  Outer-flank deployment

After deployment, the enemy can be enveloped but deployment requires time and, depending on the situation, deployment may be blocked.  The advance guard easily becomes isolated and, in cases disadvantageous for combat, slips entirely into a passive posture.

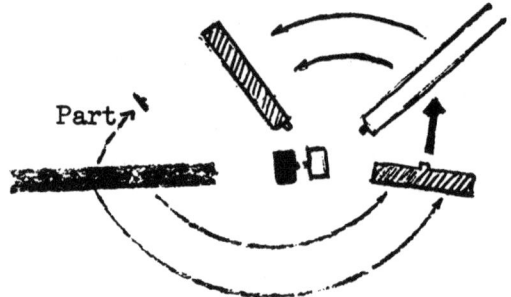

Fig. 70

    b.  Inner-flank or outer-flank deployment

In general, inner-flank deployment should be adopted.  That is because development is completed rapidly and combat power can be applied with an advantageous posture.  In this case, it is necessary that artillery be deployable and that tanks be advanced rapidly to the first line.

However, depending on terrain, position of adjacent units, etc., there are cases where adoption of exterior-flank deployment is advantageous.

Historical examples:

    Battle of Yamazaki [1582](preemption, preempting Tennō-zan hill)

    Battle near Ethe and Virton (Longwy) in the Franco-German Battles of the Frontier [August 1914] in World War I (preemptive envelopment)

    Engagement of the 12th Division near Da-yao [Ta-yao] in the Battle of Liaoyang [1904](preemption of a key position by an advance unit)

    Chapter III.  Decisive Battle Outside the Prepared Position

1.  Decisive battle outside the prepared position

    a.  A decisive battle outside the prepared position means causing the enemy who has occupied a position and is waiting for us, to abandon his position and to join in a decisive battle in terrain outside the prepared position.

b. The aim of the decisive battle outside the prepared position is to cause the enemy's abandonment of his advantage of terrain and his advantage of time (preparation), to seek a reduction in his combat power, and to hope for superiority in relative combat power.

Hence, it must be more advantageous for the enemy to leave his position than to defend in his occupied position, or the situation must be made such that he cannot continue to occupy the position.

2. Area planned for the decisive engagement outside the prepared position

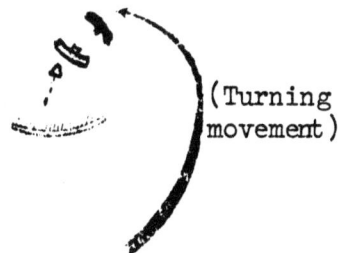

(Turning movement)

Fig. 71

   a. Rear of the enemy's position

Historical examples: The Sedan and Poland campaigns of the German Army.

   b. In front of the enemy's position

Historical example: Battle of Xu-zhou [Hsü-chou, 1938]

Luring the enemy out in front of his position

Fig. 72

3. Conditions for occurrence of the decisive battle outside the prepared position (decisive battle in the rear of the enemy's position)

   a. Establishment of a posture that can force upon the enemy a decisive engagement outside his prepared position

At a distance far enough away so that the enemy cannot use his prepared position, we effect a turning movement at a location that poses a serious threat to the enemy's line of communications.

   b. Being able to contain the enemy, that is, precluding his withdrawal to avoid a decisive engagement with us.

For this purpose, it is necessary to give consideration to such items as the following:

     (1) Rapid tactical movement to the area where the decisive engagement is expected

     (2) Concealment of our plans (actions)

     (3) It is necessary to give consideration to holding (deception, feint, dummy deployment, etc.) the enemy in his present position.

   c. Safety, reliability, and concealment of movement to the area where the decisive engagement outside the prepared position is expected to occur.

d. Ability to apply our combat power completely during the decisive engagement.

In other words, maintaining the security of our line of communications. (Selection of direction, covering action, etc.)

4. Relationship between the unit occupying the position and reinforcing (rear) units

In cases where a decisive engagement outside the prepared position is expected, it is necessary to consider not only the confronted unit occupying the position, but also the relationship to the enemy's main force. In other words, it is necessary to consider whether or not the relationship with the enemy main force that reinforces or follows in the rear is strategically adequate. It must be noted that, at times, there are cases where the enemy constructs a trap.

Fig. 73

5. The turning movement

a. The main goal of the turning movement is a decisive battle outside the prepared position

In other words, we avoid the enemy's main resistance to strike weak points deep in his flanks and rear, secure the initiative, and attempt to hold and destroy the enemy in the area we desire.

b. The turning movement has the nature of preparation to destroy the enemy.

In other words, it is a movement that is not a deep envelopment. Hence, since the turning unit usually operates beyond supporting distance from other attacking units, it must avoid being defeated in detail by the enemy and retain sufficient combat power to destroy the enemy's main force.

c. Action after the turning movement.

In regard to action after the turning movement, there is the case of joining combat directly and the case of simply seizing a concentration area and preparing for subsequent action.

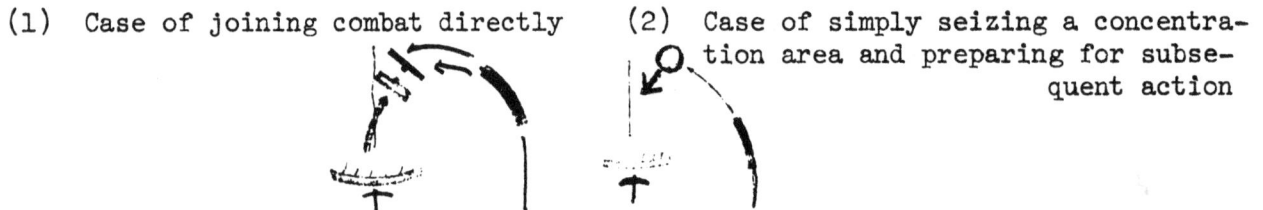

(1) Case of joining combat directly

(2) Case of simply seizing a concentration area and preparing for subsequent action

Fig. 74

d. Like the enveloping force being enveloped, it is necessary for the force executing a turning movement to be sufficiently careful not to be subjected to a turning movement, and to prepare countermeasures.

Historical examples:

The Inchon Landing in the Korean War [September 1950]

The turning movement of Ulm [1805]

## Chapter IV.  Interdiction of the Rear

1. Value of interdiction of the rear

a. If its rear is interdicted, usually the unit has its route of withdrawal interdicted, and it cannot get supplies and collapses.  Also, it is easily isolated and annihilated.

b. Interdiction of its rear, for the enemy force, is a reason for withdrawal. In other words, it provides an inducement for recognizing defeat.

The cause of withdrawal in defeat —

- With a small unit:
  - Includes directly received materiel losses,
  - And also a threat to the rear that arouses the instinct for disengagement.
- With a large unit:
  - The more important the supply, the greater the threat to the rear;
  - The connecting lines of leadership are cut, and replacements are interrupted.

In other words, if it is a large unit, the situation of posture disadvantage, that is, of strategic disadvantage, rather than materiel losses, is the inducement for withdrawal.

[1] When there is complete encirclement, however, bravery comes to the fore.

This action also is produced merely by presenting a threat to the rear (route of withdrawal), and there occurs a strictly strategic effect.

[2] "Without fighting, to surrender to enemy forces" is because of the good of the soldiers (Sun-zi [Sun-tzŭ]).

In any case, the rear (route of withdrawal) ordinarily develops a weak point because of the disposition of the enemy, and this weak point itself naturally becomes a tactical objective.

2. What is the nature of the rear (route of withdrawal)?

It is necessary to clarify the meaning of terms related to this.

a.  Line of communications

It means the group of transportation routes (roads, railroads, water routes, air routes,
etc.) that connects an operating
force with its base of operations (base for activity and
subsistence that the operating
force has in its rear) or
logistic support area.

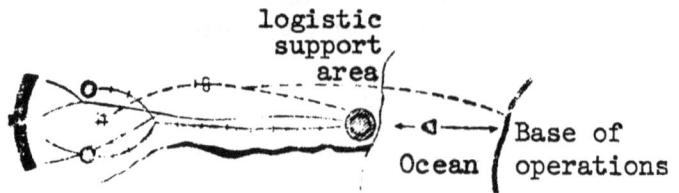

Fig. 75

In other words, the operating force is maintained and strengthened mainly by the
lines of communications.

b.  The withdrawal route also justifiably may be considered to be generally
identical with the line of communications.

However, in military history, there also are many cases in which the actual
withdrawal route, not only when forced by the enemy but also when freely adopted,
is different in direction from the original line of communications.

c.  In connection with the lines of communications, there are the following
principles:

(1)  The force must never allow its lines of communications to be
threatened.

(2)  Change of the lines of communications is extremely difficult if the
force is large.  Hence, it is effected only in cases where necessary for the security of the force.

Note:  Interdiction of the rear, as noted above, includes interdiction of the
route of withdrawal, interdiction of supply routes, splitting up and isolation
of the rear, etc., but the text below speaks principally concerning the
essentials of interdicting the route of withdrawal.

3.  Essentials of interdicting the route of withdrawal

a.  Among the essentials of interdicting the route of withdrawal are the
method of directly attacking the withdrawal route with a part of the force (or
the main force)(envelopment, turning movement, tactical air movement, etc.) and
various methods such as attack by guerrillas, aircraft, etc., but here are discussed principally the items that require attention in determining the direction
of attack.

b.  Strategic and tactical considerations for determining the direction
of attack

(1)  Determining the direction of attack must be considered from both
the strategic and the tactical viewpoint.

Strategically {
Area that can interdict the enemy's withdrawal route

Area that permits operating on exterior lines

- - - → (Envelopment → interdiction of the withdrawal route)

Tactically {
Enemy's weak point

- - - - → (Rear also is one of the weak points)

Area where application of our combat power is easy

In other words, considered from both the strategic and the tactical viewpoint, the main attack is directed toward the area that is most advantageous for the situation at that time.

(2)  Case of the breakthrough

The enemy is split and pressed and destroyed away from his original line of communications.

Maginot Line breakthrough (10-21 May 1940)

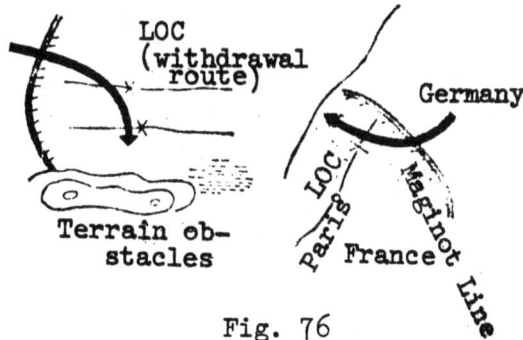

Fig. 76

(3)  Envelopment (turning movement)

The wing to be enveloped is selected in the area passing through a vital part of the enemy, that is, his line of communications.

Rommel's envelopment (turning movement) of Gazala (27 May-13 June 1942)

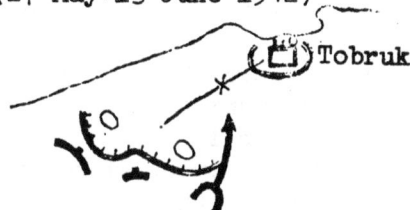

Fig. 77

(4) Pursuit

Besides envelopment and a turning movement, a breakthrough is effected and the enemy's route of withdrawal is quickly interdicted.

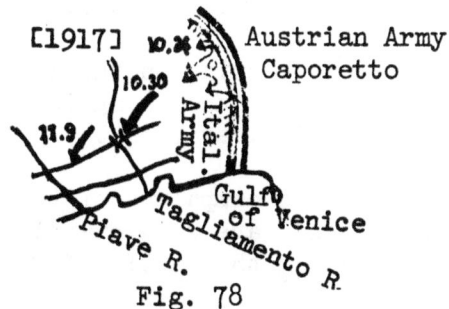

Fig. 78

c. Items that should be considered in determining the direction of attack

(1) The withdrawal route is cut in an acute angle

With B, as the battle front pulls back, our line of operations is parallel to the route of withdrawal, and interception is not possible.

A, on the other hand, is close and interdicts easily.

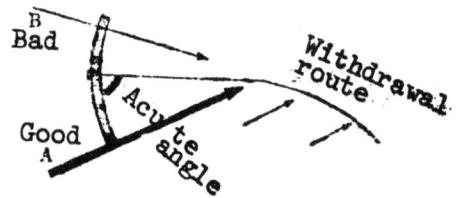

Fig. 79

(2) Essentials of pressing [the enemy] toward a terrain obstacle

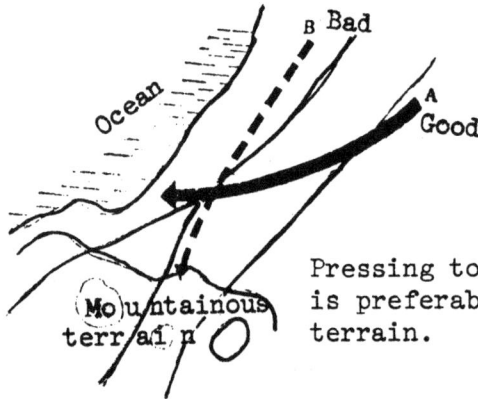

Pressing toward the ocean or a large river is preferable to pressing against mountainous terrain.

Fig. 80

(3) Interdiction of air movement is necessary.

In modern warfare, air logistics is highly developed, and there are cases where, even when there is interdiction of surface supply lines, effectiveness is slight.

Air superiority has overwhelming power in interdicting lines of communications. Also, low-altitude operations or landings by enemy aircraft can be limited or made impossible by antiaircraft firepower. (Da Nang, Dien Bien Phu, etc.)

Fig. 81

(4) Necessitating control of the sea

In land operations backing on the sea, if control of the sea and air is gained [by the enemy], the ground being defended must be abandoned without fighting. (Interdiction of withdrawal route)

In World War II, the campaigns of the Japanese Army on the Asiatic continent and on South Sea islands are good examples; and in the Russo-Japanese War, if Japan had been defeated in the Battle of Tsushima, a similar outcome probably would have resulted.

      (5) Other

If a large unit holds terrain in its rear, even if there is an envelopment, if the route of withdrawal is not completely interdicted, disengagement is easy to accomplish.

In the Russo-Japanese War, the Battle of Mukden is a good example of this.

If there seems to be a change in the ratio of relative combat power, the hitherto attacker must consolidate his posture or, at an appropriate time, change to the defensive; and the defender must create or seize a favorable tactical opportunity and, at a suitable time, change to the offensive and seek to destroy the enemy.

2. Cause of occurrence of a turning point in the course of a battle

    a. Distance from the base of operations

For the attacker, maintenance and increase in combat power become difficult from extending the line of communications, and his combat power is caused to decrease. On the other hand, for the defender, the line of communications is shortened, increase in combat power becomes easier, and combat power increases.

<u>Historical examples</u>:

    Napoleon's Moscow Campaign

    Operations in the south-
    east Pacific area in World
    War II

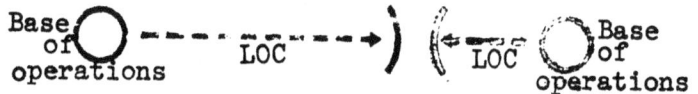

Fig. 82

    German operations against the Soviet Union in World War II

    Operations of the North Korean Army in the Korean War until the Pusan beachhead

<u>Note</u>: Such situations frequently occur in the conduct of a war or in operations of large units (strategic level). At the tactical level, this type of situation develops in the stage of exploitation, pursuit, etc.

    b. Change in superiority in combat power

      (1) Buildup of combat power

The buildup of combat power of the defender is superior to that of the attacker.

        (a) Reinforcement

        (b) Improvement in rear-area posture

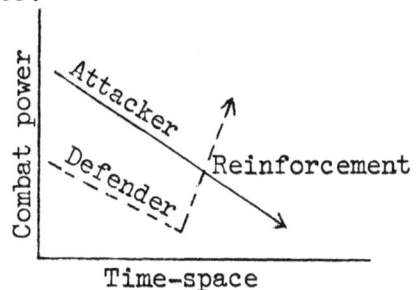

Fig. 83

Part VI.  LIMIT OF COMBAT POWER

Chapter I.  Calculation of the Turning Point in a Battle

Section 1.  Summary

1.  Meaning of the turning point in a battle

   a.  The turning point in a battle is the point where a situation occurs that causes a change in the respective posture and combat power of each of the two sides so that there is a reversal in the ratio of relative combat power, or the point at which the conduct of tactical operations changes to an advantageous situation.

In this case, the point where the situation reverses the ratio of relative combat power is called "the turnabout point in combat power."

   b.  Since the turning point in a battle generally has the result of reversing the positions of attack and defense, judging the timeliness and appropriateness of a turning point in a battle and a plan to cope with it are extremely important, and when there is an error in this, a severe defeat results.

   (2)[sic]  Reduction in combat power from attrition

The combat power of the attacker decreases faster than that of the defender and becomes equal to, or lower than, that of the defender.

      (a)  There is great probability of a gradual decrease in offensive power in cases where there initially is no great difference in the ratio of combat power of the two parties.

      (b)  Attrition of the combat power of the attacker is greater than that of the defender.

      (c)  The decrease in combat power of the attacker includes unit fatigue, disadvantage of posture, and the influence of terrain, weather, etc.

   c.  Dispersion and expansion of the battle line

The attacker, in order to contain the defender, necessarily disperses and extends his battle line, and the attack power on individual unit fronts is caused to decrease below the combat power of the defender.

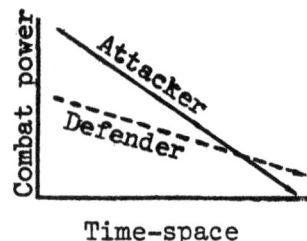

Time-space

Fig. 84

Section 2.  Counteroffensive

1.  Meaning of counteroffensive

Counteroffensive means a unit that is in a defensive position shifting to the offensive in order to advance and deliver a decisive blow to the enemy, the action of the unit that shifts to the offensive being an all-out attack with the objective of overwhelming and annihilating the enemy.

Combat, by its nature, can reach its objective only by the offensive (attack). Hence, the defender, on seeing an opportunity, shifts to the offensive (attack), there is constant effort to seize tactical opportunities to destroy the enemy, and this course can be seen in many historical examples.

Historical examples:

> Counteroffensive of the Japanese Army in the Battle of Sha-he [Sha-ho] in the Russo-Japanese War

> Counteroffensive of the combined forces of Oda and Tokugawa in the Battle of Nagashino [1575]

2. Conditions for a counteroffensive

For a counteroffensive, it is necessary to rely on a turnabout in relative combat power and on superior posture.

a. Turnabout in relative combat power

See this chapter, Section 1.

b. Superior posture

(1) The enemy is decoyed into an unfavorable posture. (Decoy attack)

The enemy being drawn into our snare (for example, within a reentrant in our position) and being caused to assume a disadvantageous posture, seems to be a definitely correct course of action, but whether or not the enemy accepts it depends on the enemy's will.

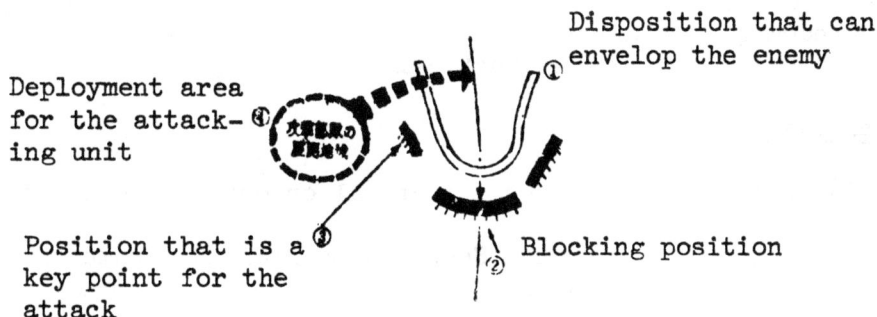

Fig. 85. Example of a desirable posture

Hence, in decoying the enemy, reliance must be placed, inter alia, on the following:

> (a) The enemy is caused to take the course of action that is most desirable in his situation

    (b)  A lure (bait) is provided.

    (c)  Forcing in accordance with the over-all posture.

Decoying with dummy troop dispositions, unnatural small works, etc., is an unreasonable requirement, and when this is a prerequisite in plans for a counteroffensive, failure may occur.

    (2)  Taking advantage of enemy mistakes

Mistakes are an accompaniment of combat, and there are many cases of inviting a disadvantageous posture through mistakes.  However, this is a chance occurrence, and it is not reasonable to expect this from the beginning, but the commander must have the insight to discover this tactical opportunity quickly and take advantage of it.

Historical example:  Battle of the French Second Army on the banks of the Meurthe River in World War I [20-22 August 1914].

Note:  In regard to the "retrograde offensive":  This is the action of a with-drawing unit in turning the momentum of the pursuing unit against that force and shifting to the counterattack, and it succeeds only through a major mistake by the pursuing unit.

Historical example:  Battle of the German Sixth Army in Lorraine in World War I.

3.  Time of shift to the offensive

    a.  Possibility of a shift to the offensive

The possibility of a shift to the offensive varies from moment to moment because of the enemy's changes in posture (shifting to the defensive, adjustments in posture, etc.).  Moreover, if the shift to the offensive is not accomplished at the time the possibility is most opportune, there are many cases where, not only is the desired result not realizable, but it ends in failure and the tactical situation becomes disadvantageous.  Hence, it is extremely important and also difficult to seize a favorable tactical opportunity in shifting to the offensive.

Historical examples:

    (1)  Examples of missing a tactical opportunity and failing

        Battle of the French Second Army near "Ryūurumu" on the banks of the Meurthe River [August 1914]

        Battle of the French Third Army and the Army of Lorraine on the banks of the Haute Aisne [20-22 August 1914]

    (2)  Examples of properly seizing an opportunity and achieving success

        Offensive of the German Eighth Army (François's Corps) in the Battle of Gumbinnen

Joffre's offensive in the Battle of the Marne [1914]

The offensive of the Japanese Army at the Sha-he [Sha-ho (Manchuria)][battle, 1904]

b.  Ideal time to shift to the offensive

   (1)  Containing enemy momentum at a key front, with us having the advantage in posture

   (2)  The combat power of the enemy being greatly reduced, at the time of turnabout [in the balance] of combat power of the attacker and defender

   (3)  Time when offensive combat power is sufficient and preparations for an offensive have been completed

c.  Time of implementing a shift to the offensive

   (1)  In cases where concentration of forces or arrival of reinforcing units is made the occasion for shifting to the offensive, discovering the opportunity is easy, but in cases of taking advantage of a setback in an enemy attack or of an enemy mistake, the commander must have an excellent eye for opportunities.

   (2)  A moderate amount of time is required from the decision to the execution of a shift to the offensive.  (If the unit is large, [the time] is really long.)  Hence, during this period, changes in the tactical situation, such as how the tactical opportunity may change and whether the key front may not collapse, are appropriately discerned, and the time is determined for carrying out the change to the offensive.

   (3)  In preparation for the action of a change to the offensive, the minimum required condition is completion of deployment of artillery forces.

For example, it is the time when artillery that is deployed in depth has completed deployment laterally.  Also, this is an indication for judging the time of an opponent's action changing to the offensive.

Also, in regard to a shift to the offensive, it must not be forgotten that close air support also is an important condition.

Fig. 86

4.  Direction of a shift to the offensive

Determination of the direction of an attack, along with selection of the proper moment for making an attack, exerts an important influence on the success of a shift to the offensive.  It is desirable to select the following in the light of an estimate of changes in the tactical situation between the decision and implementation.

a.  Ability to envelop simultaneously units both on the flank and in the rear of the enemy.

b.  Optimum direction relative to a subsequent attack by units of the key front.

Historical examples:

Battle of Gumbinnen (A) (suitable)

Battle of the Arges River [Romania, August 1916-February 1917] (B) (unsuitable)

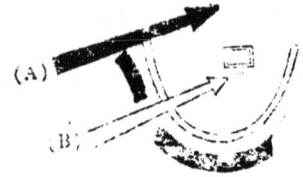

Fig. 87

5.  Relationship between the key front and the decisive engagement

Example of the relationship between the key-front position and the main-decision battlefield in cases of an attack toward an unsupported flank of the enemy force

a.  Case in which the main-decision battlefield is abreast of the key front or behind its flank

In this case, there is little strategic gain along the enemy's line of communications, and decisive results cannot be obtained, but implementation is easy.

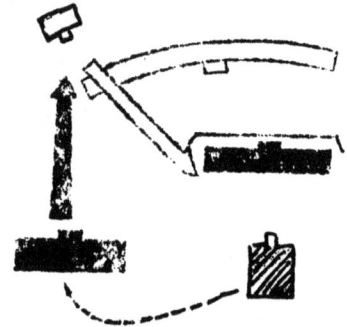

Fig. 88

b.  Case in which the main decisive battle is sought in front of a flank of the key front

In this case, if successful, there is great possibility of containing the enemy unit, and a great victory can be gained, but there are the following problems concerning implementation:

(1)  Since deployment is within the enemy's power sphere, reaching the attack position is dangerous.

Fig. 89

(2)  The flanks and rear of the attacking unit are exposed and particularly subject to enemy attack.

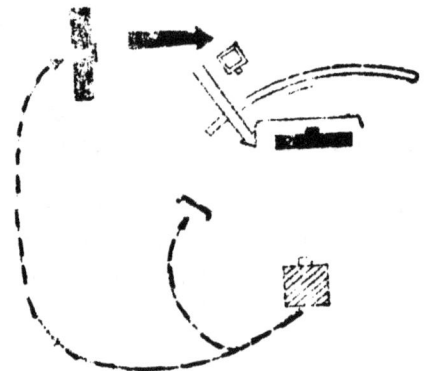

Historical example:

Offensive of the French Third Army on the river banks of the Haute Aisne [20-22 August 1914]

From the above two examples:

Case a. is easy and safe to carry out, but has small results.

Case b. is extremely dangerous but, if successful, has large results. (Relationship between risk and results)

The question of which to adopt depends solely upon the situation but, in particular, is governed by the self-confidence of the commander.

6. The shift to the offensive effected toward an enemy flank from a salient in the battle line

This is using the undulations of the battle line; interdicting, from a salient in it, the withdrawal route of the enemy element that has advanced into a reentrant; and attempting to destroy that force.

Fig. 90

This method being a breakthrough, its conditions are primarily careful preparation and concentration of superior decisive combat power. However, in actuality, even if the undulations are produced in the battle line and a reentrant is formed, since the enemy holds the initiative and undulations in the battle line are ever-changing, there are many cases of losing the moment of tactical opportunity. Hence, in history, there are many examples of shifting to the offensive in current posture without completing preparations, and failing.

Historical examples:

Battle of the French Third Army on the river banks of the Haute Aisne [20-22 August 1914]

Battle of the Austrian Fourth Army in the vicinity of "Rimanowa [Limanowa?]"-"Rabanowa" [Battle of Komarow (1914)?]

7. Offensive defense (decisive defense)

Offensive defense means defense which, from the first, plans an offensive, seeking to shift to the offensive when an opportunity is found, in order to attempt a decisive battle.

For example, in cases where we have an offensive mission and it would be disadvantageous to assume the offensive immediately because of the relationship between the combat power of the two sides or because of posture, we temporarily assume the defensive, impose casualties on the enemy, and after making the ratio of relative combat power of the two sides favorable to us or creating a posture advantageous to us, attempt to shift to the offensive.

In this case, defensive dispositions and the conduct of defensive combat must be structured with the primary purpose of the offensive. Since this defense is combat that involves a special requirement on the enemy, and since the enemy has free will, it is necessary always to give strict attention to impose our desired course.

<u>Historical examples:</u>

Napoleon's Battle of Austerlitz [1805]

Masayuki Sanada's Battle of Ueda [1600?]

### Section 3.  Offensive's termination point

1.  Meaning of the offensive's termination point

The offensive's termination point is the point where the attacker reaches the limit of offensive capability, which depends on the extending of the battle line, lengthening of the supply line, materiel shortages, etc.

2.  Estimate of the offensive's termination point

When past military history and historical examples are examined, there are very many examples of mistakes in estimating the offensive's termination point and suffering major defeats; hence, one can know how important this estimate is.

   a.  Relationship to the combat-situation (combat-capability) tur about point

The offensive's termination point generally is sought before the combat-capability turnabout point.  Hence, in regard to relative combat power, in situations where superiority can be maintained, it is necessary to conduct subsequent operations.

In other words, it can be said to be a situation where it is advantageous to have a turnabout  in the conduct of military operations, a turning point in the battle.

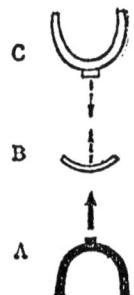

Fig. 91

   b.  One example of the offensive's termination point in the tactical sphere

<u>Example:</u>  A > B, A < C
             A is attacking B, and B is gradually withdrawing.
             C is advancing, and its time of arrival is the time at
               which A can completely defeat B.

Consideration of this case while disregarding other factors:

   Case of "1" [in Fig. 92]

[Force] A can defeat B, but at that point in time, C arrives on the battlefield. The combat power of A is reduced by attrition, posture also collapses, and conflict with C is extremely disadvantageous.

Case of "2" [in Fig. 92]

[Force] A cannot completely defeat B, a considerable part remaining, but A obtains a margin to cope with C.

Case of "3" [in Fig. 92]

[Force] A obtains sufficient margin of time to cope with C, but, in this case, A must cope with C and the remaining part of B (a still respectable combat power).

In this case, it may be concluded that "2" would be suitable as the offensive's termination point for A.

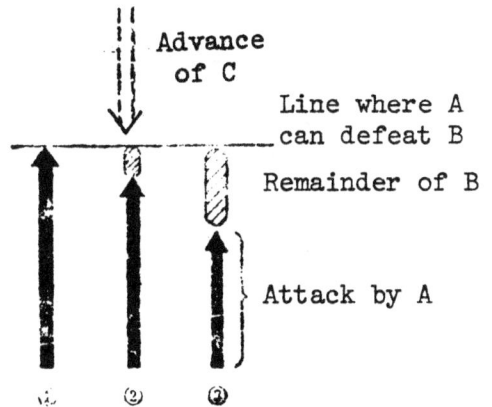

Fig. 92

In actual cases, the estimate must be made on the basis of the time when C advances and of the terrain in the vicinity of the battlefield, the limit of our combat power, the degree of effect of the defeat and withdrawal of B on C, etc.

Historical example:

Battle of Napoleon in the vicinity of Lake Garda [1796?]. (It is an example in which, during the pursuit, the limit of the offensive was seized while remaining on the defensive, and the Austrian Army was defeated in detail.)

3. Luring into entrapment toward the offensive's termination point

For the defender to lure the attacker into entrapment past the offensive's termination point toward the combat-power turnabout point, there are the following essentials:

a. The terrain is utilized to extend the enemy's combat power in depth or laterally.

b. The enemy's posture is split, and his supply, etc., are blocked or interdicted.

c. Exhaustion of the enemy's base of operations is sought.

Historical examples:

Competition in extending the flank in the Battle of the Marne in World War I

Counteroffensive of the U.S. forces against the Japanese in World War II

[German] counterattack at Avranches [France, 6-10 August 1944], counteroffensive of Soviet forces against Germany, etc.

## Section 4.  Vying in extending a flank and in enveloping

1.  Meaning of vying in extending a flank and in enveloping

    a.  Vying in extending a flank and in enveloping means a maneuver in which, during combat, both forces each seek a decisive victory by extending the respective facing flank and effecting an envelopment.

Vying in extending a flank and in enveloping occurs on open flanks or in gaps in the battle line; and when it occurs at gaps, joint action with adjacent units is evoked.

    b.  Vying in extending a flank and in enveloping causes successive piecemeal application of combat power, expansion of the battle line, unit fatigue, etc., and when there is lapse into these, obtaining a decisive victory becomes increasingly difficult.

Historical examples:

    Vying between German and French forces in extending open flanks in the Battle of Flanders in World War I

    Extending gap flanks by the Austrian and Russian forces in the battle of "Rimanofu [Limanowa?]"-"Rabanofu" [Battle of Komarow?] in World War I

In all of these, if the stage of decisive victory is not gained, it is not a desirable situation.

2.  Estimate of the turning point in the battle, in vying in extending a flank and in enveloping

    a.  Against our envelopment, the enemy carries out a counterenvelopment, and in cases of expected occurrence of this type of vying in extending a flank, it is necessary to discern properly the turning point in the battle and to make a proper judgment of the time and place that a decisive victory should be sought.

    b.  Items which must be considered in order to estimate the turning point in the battle are unit casualties, degree of fatigue, supply situation, tactical mobility, collection of intelligence information, degree of air superiority, etc.

    c.  Plan to seek a decisive victory in cases where a counterenvelopment is undertaken in response to an envelopment.

Example:

Below, when the enemy carries out a counterenvelopment against our envelopment, the vying is avoided and we consider how we can achieve a decisive victory.

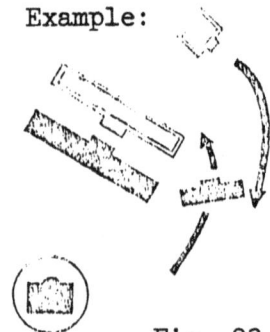

    (1)  Attack against the enemy's axis of envelopment [Fig. 94]

The battle line that is being enveloped by the enemy is curved or moved back, the enemy is temporarily

Fig. 93

blocked, decisive combat power is concentrated, and the enemy's axis of
envelopment or flank is attacked.

In this case, it is necessary to cause
the enemy to extend his flank on an exterior line and we on an interior line
and, by this means, to maintain the
balance.

Also, at this time, it is necessary to
accept a disadvantageous tactical situation for a certain time.

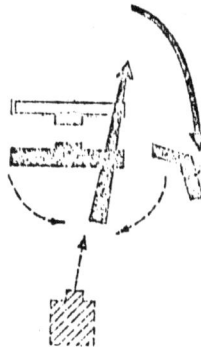
Fig. 94

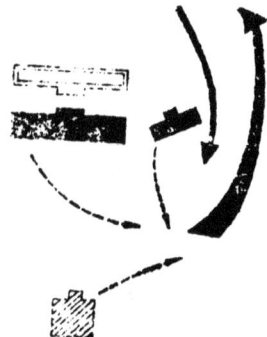
Fig. 95

(2)  Counterenvelopment [Fig. 95]

Concentrating our decisive combat power, we carry out the counterenvelopment.
At that time, it is necessary that there be a great and powerful action seeking
to envelop also the enemy's entire reserve, so as to frustrate enemy plans for
subsequent envelopment.

Whether to adopt the measure to attack the enemy's axis of envelopment or to
carry out a counterenvelopment must depend on discerning the turning point in
the battle and properly judging the time and place to seek a decisive victory.

Chapter II.  Pursuit and Retrograde Movement

Section 1.  Pursuit

1.  Meaning of pursuit

Pursuit is one form of attack carried out in order to destroy enemy forces that
are disengaging (withdrawing) from the battlefield, and its basic character is
an engagement and not a maneuver.

2.  Necessity of pursuit

a.  In a situation where pursuit is necessary, if we consider the actions
which the enemy can take in case we do not carry out a pursuit, they are as
follows:

(1)  The enemy withdraws safely.  Hence, we cannot make up for losses
received at the time of an attack.

(2)  The enemy corrects his posture and restores discipline.  In other
words, the enemy is able to reestablish a posture of being able to
oppose us.

(3)  The enemy stops at the place he desires and carries out preparation
for subsequent resistance undisturbed.

(4) Combat power is increased through recovery from fatigue and getting closer to his base of operations.

b. Disadvantages to us from not carrying out a pursuit, in addition to the above, are as follows:

(1) Advantages considered achievable by pursuit are missed.

(2) In order to make another attack, new sacrifices must be made.

c. Situation of losses by both sides

(1) Attack on a position

Our losses are large, and the losses of the defending enemy are small.

(2) Pursuit

Our losses are small, and the losses of the withdrawing enemy are large.

From the above, the victor must lose no opportunity, disregard all difficulties, and carry out a pursuit.

In the Russo-Japanese War, because the Japanese Army did not pursue after the Battle of Liao-yang, the Russian Army made a stand in the vicinity of Mukden and, moreover, turned back, shifted to the offensive, and there occurred the subsequent Battle of Sha-he [Sha-ho]; and this bluntly states the necessity of pursuit.

Also, one should remember the wise words of Moltke expressing the necessity of the pursuit, saying, "For purposes of pursuit, as long as the men and horses of the pursuing force have the spirit to pursue and the enemy does not surrender to this pressure, pursuit must not be stopped, regardless of whether the enemy may have sufficient spirit to continue advancing, and there is no reason for us not to have it."

2. Difficulty of carrying out a pursuit

a. There are extremely few historical examples of successful pursuits in the past. This fact speaks bluntly of the difficulty of carrying out a pursuit.

b. The following are considered to be causes of the difficulty in carrying out a pursuit:

(1) Feeling of satisfaction in victory produced by the enemy's withdrawal

(2) Fatigue of body and mind

(3) Error in judgment by the front-line commander concerning pursuit, because of uncertainty about the general situation

(4) Being restricted by losses and by correction of posture

(5) Nighttime

(6) Weather influences, terrain obstacles, shortage of organic equipment

(7) Enemy counteractions and uncertainty of the enemy situation

(8) Supply and rear-area situation

3. Conditions for instituting a pursuit

a. Our posture being advantageous at the time of change to the pursuit.

b. Clearly stating plans relative to the pursuit, preparing early pursuit, and the initial action of the pursuit being advantageous relative to the general situation.

c. Quickly perceiving the initial action of the enemy's withdrawal and immediately taking advantage of it.

d. Pressing and containing the withdrawing enemy on his front. (Contact with the enemy must not be lost.)

4. Conduct of the pursuit

Items which must receive maximum attention in order to intercept and destroy the enemy by pursuit are as follows:

Where to have the pursuit objective?

How to have the positioning (direction) for pursuit?

a. Pursuit objective

It is necessary to select [an objective] on the terrain line where the enemy can be intercepted. Its remoteness varies with the enemy's withdrawal situation. If the enemy can be intercepted nearby, that is most ideal, but where reliable interception nearby is not possible, a maximum effort must be made to select a distant objective.

b. Positioning (direction) for pursuit

It is difficult to intercept and destroy the enemy by merely following the enemy withdrawing from his front and carrying out a pursuit, and it is necessary to push in from the enemy's flank and carry out a pursuit toward the enemy's rear.

In other words, it is necessary to be positioned so that the pursuit is carried out from a broad front.

c. In view of the above, in order to intercept and destroy the enemy, pursuit must be carried out over a wide and deep area.

d.  Making pursuit constriction effective

(Pursuit constriction is the angle of intersection of the line of direction of
the unit pushing in from the flank [unit given the mission of effecting a turning movement], with the axis of withdrawal of the enemy)

(1)  In many cases in military history, one
major cause of letting the enemy escape is being
dazzled by the immediate battle situation (enemy's
retreat situation) and shortsightedly sharply
changing the direction of pursuit by the unit pushing in from the flank, [so the direction is] toward
the enemy's flank and rear, in order quickly to
interdict the route of withdrawal.

[In Fig. 96] pursuit toward A is wrong (the enemy
is allowed to escape, because when we have reached
point A, the enemy will be withdrawing to line C).

Pursuit must be toward B.

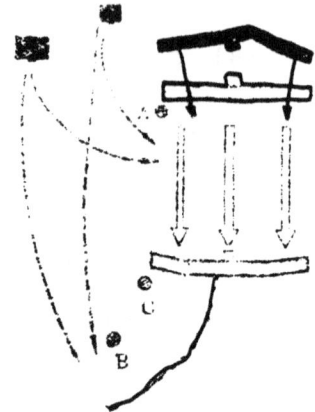

Fig. 96

(2)  Considerations concerning the remoteness
of the pursuit constriction

In cases where, as in the Battle of Tannenberg, the enemy himself also has great
confidence in victory, attempts an advance toward us to attack, decides to withdraw from a disadvantageous encircled posture by a sudden change in strategic
posture from a rather deep engagement situation, and his withdrawal is greatly
limited because of us, pursuit that interdicts the enemy's withdrawal route at
a relatively close location (pursuit with nearby constriction) is best.

In contrast, in general, even if an enemy on the defensive is still only slight-
ly engaged in combat, in case our created advantageous strategic posture is seen
and an attempt at timely withdrawal is made in order to escape from us, it must
be borne in mind that attempting nearby interdiction of the enemy's withdrawal
route (pursuit with nearby constriction), in many cases, becomes the reason for
the enemy's escape.

(3)  Items which require care in carrying out an effective constriction
in a pursuit, are as follows:

(a)  Correctly estimating the enemy's withdrawal direction.

(b)  Accurately estimating the time that the enemy begins the
withdrawal.

(c)  Considering the relationship with our offensive's termination
point.

e.  Since enemy units to be intercepted in a pursuit disappear, appropriate
countermeasures against this are necessary.

Historical examples:

(1) Examples of successful pursuit

Napoleon's distant pushing in from a flank in a pursuit following the Battle of Jena [1806]

The Malay Campaign

(2) Examples of unsuccessful pursuit

The Japanese Army's Battle of Liao-yang [1904] in the Russo-Japanese War

The German Army's pursuit toward Dunkirk in World War II

(3) Example of the enemy disappearing during the pursuit

Disappearance of the North Korean Army in the Korean War

## Section 2.  Retrograde movement

1.  Meaning of retrograde movement

Retrograde movement is stopping the current engagement and withdrawing toward the rear in order to conform to a new operations plan.

Attack, defense, pursuit, and the delaying action are combat engagements, whereas the basic nature of the retrograde movement lies in its being an evolution.

The delaying action and retrograde movement both aim at giving terrain to the enemy and gaining time, but differ in whether combat power is used.

2.  Primary objective of the retrograde movement

The primary objective of the retrograde movement is to separate quickly from the enemy.

Hence, except when absolutely unavoidable, it is necessary to correct posture quickly without engaging in combat with the enemy, and withdraw toward an objective.

3.  Determination of the retrograde movement's objective

If it has been decided to execute a retrograde movement, it is necessary, based upon the subsequent operations plan, to select an objective of the retrograde movement in a location sufficiently distant to gain a time margin at least to correct posture.

The main factors influencing selection of the retrograde movement's objective are as follows:

a.  The forward-movement capability of the logistic support of the pursuing force [i.e., capability of logistic support to keep up with movements of combat elements]

b. Degree to which the transportation lines used by the pursuing force can be destroyed.

c. Degree of delay of the pursuit that is progressively increased by the organized resistance of the rear guard.

d. Degree of preparation for the retrograde movement (if preparations are complete, even if an objective is selected that is relatively close, the goal of "separation from the enemy" can be achieved).

4. Disengagement and retirement

In order to effect a retrograde movement, it is necessary first to break contact with the enemy (disengagement) and then to gain space from the enemy (retirement).

Also, with disengagement and retirement, there are cases that are carried out voluntarily and cases carried out because forced by the enemy.

a. Disengagement

(1) Main factors affecting the difficulty of a disengagement are as follows:

(a) Situation of both sides. In particular:

Degree of pressure from the enemy

Existence of our reserves and fresh troops

Relationship between the front line and the line of communications (angle of enemy interdiction of our line of withdrawal)

(b) Terrain

(c) Time of disengagement (especially whether daytime or nighttime)

(d) Weather

(2) Method of disengagement in cases where our line of withdrawal may be cut in an acute angle [Fig. 97]

(3) Measures to facilitate disengagement

(a) Repulsing the enemy or dealing a major blow to the enemy

(b) Local counterattack

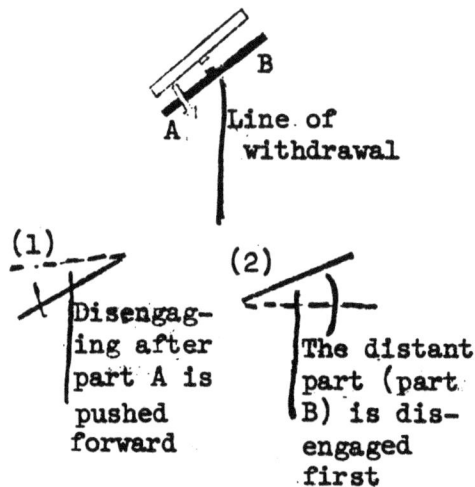

Line of withdrawal

(1) Disengaging after part A is pushed forward

(2) The distant part (part B) is disengaged first

Fig. 97

- 102 -

The enemy's attack plan is frustrated, he is placed temporarily on the defensive, and meanwhile, taking advantage of this interval, we accomplish disengagement. However, there are many cases where it is difficult to place the entire enemy force on the defensive with a local counterattack. A counter-attack when a retrograde movement is intended, is the ultimate measure in cases of an unavoidable situation.

### (c) Use of nighttime

Daytime disengagement, except in cases of unavoidable situations, must be avoided as much as possible.

### (d) Use of terrain

Since, because of the terrain, one element of the force is easy for the enemy to press and [another] element is difficult to press, units in the element that is difficult to press because of the terrain, cover the disengagement of units in the other element.

### (e) An element which, because of local pressure, would cause another element to become difficult to disengage, is directed to resist desperately.

### (f) Use of weather

It involves a large element of chance, but there are examples of its successful use.

### (4) Sequence of disengagement of front-line units

Disengagement is from places where enemy pressure is slight. However, depending upon terrain and the relationship to the line of withdrawal, there are cases where units under heavy enemy pressure are dis-engaged first.

For example, the following cases are of this type:

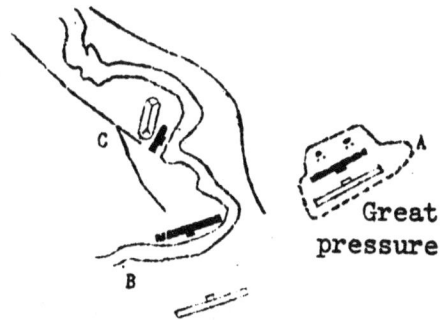

Fig. 98

Even though there is a breakthrough at A, the enemy cannot advance rapidly while there exists a covering position at C.

However, when there is a disengagement at B, there is danger that the enemy will exert direct pressure on the line of withdrawal, disengagement at A will become increasingly difficult, and C may even become unusable.

Hence, in this case, disengagement is from A.

b. Retirement

    (1) Increase in relative evolution capability

It is necessary to increase our evolution capability, reduce the enemy's evolution capability, and attempt to increase [our] relative evolution capability.

        (a) Use of the maximum total tactical mobility (transport capability)

        (b) Obstruction of enemy pursuit

            1 Use of terrain, especially of obstructions

            2 Delaying, by air assault, the advance of the enemy

    (2) Direction of retrograde movement

The direction of retrograde movement generally is selected on the basis of our line of communications; but, depending upon the situation, a different direction may be selected. Below are a number of considerations concerning the direction of retrograde movement.

        (a) At the time of deciding upon a retrograde movement, in a situation where the enemy is advancing his posture of pushing in and enveloping from the flank, it being impossible to withdraw in one's desired direction, initially, as a precondition to escaping the enemy's envelopment, the retrograde movement temporarily is in a direction far from the line of communications. (Retrograde movement that describes an arc)

In this case, it is necessary to secure the vicinity of the axis of maneuver and to surpass the enemy in tactical mobility.

        (b) Depending upon the situation and terrain, there are cases where it is not possible to withdraw in the direction of one's own base of operations, and the line of withdrawal must be changed.

In this case, the key to success is whether it is possible to ensure supply.

        (c) Centrifugal retrograde movement [=retrograde movement dispersing on radial lines that permit return to the original central point]

The centrifugal retrograde movement is carried out in the following cases:

Retrograde movement after a breakthrough in the center by the enemy

On the basis of a position relative to the terrain, particularly to the battlefield and to cover

A retrograde movement with the purpose of decoying the enemy

This type of retrograde movement is good in that it causes the enemy to divide his force or operate on interior lines and we operate on exterior lines and make strategic surprise attacks, but it has the disadvantages that concealment of plans is difficult and our force is caused to be divided.

Historical example:  Retrograde movement of the German Army from the vicinity of Warsaw in World War I.

(d)  Centripetal retrograde movement

It is advantageous for establishing control over the force and reassuming the offensive, but inter-unit coordination may be bad, and there is the danger of being intercepted when the pursuing force is superior.

Historical example:  Retrograde movement of the Allied forces from the frontier to the Marne line in World War I.

5.  Measures against pursuit by the enemy pushing in from the flank

In the usual sequence of withdrawal (first the rear echelons, then the combat echelon), there is the danger of interception, or of interdiction of our route of withdrawal, by the enemy.  Hence, it is necessary to send out a highly mobile unit in front of the withdrawal route as advance guard or flank guard, or to occupy key tactical positions on the flank and in the rear, or to assume a disposition of mobile protection to the flank and rear, and then shift to withdrawal of rear elements followed by the combat echelon.

Depending upon the situation, counterattacks are made in necessary areas.

6.  Items that require particular attention in a retrograde movement

In a retrograde movement, items that require attention are utilization of terrain and weather, use of evolution capability, effective control and direction, all-around security, use of obstructions, air support, etc., but from the characteristics of the retrograde maneuver, particularly important items are the following:

Secrecy and deception concerning plans

Arousal of fighting spirit

At that time, an effort must be made particularly not to slip into a rout psychology.

Historical examples:

Operation of Sakurai's corps extricating itself from Burma

Retrograde movement of the [Japanese] 33d Division in Burma

Part VII.   OPERATIONS IN SPECIAL TERRAIN, ETC.

Chapter I.   Summary

1.   Meaning of operations in special terrain, etc.

Operations in special terrain, etc., means operations (battles) that must be given special consideration in implementation, dependent upon special operational conditions from the special nature of the operational terrain, operational time, etc.   This Part VII discusses operations that require consideration because of the special nature of the zone of operations, such as operations (battles) in mountainous terrain, river areas, defiles, forests, and populated places and in cold and snowy areas, and operations that require consideration because of the special nature of the timing of the operations, such as operations that utilize nighttime darkness, etc.

2.   Application of these principles of war

The principles of war discussed in this Part VII, in contrast to the items discussed in Parts II-VI, are those principles which should be additionally applied or modified under specified conditions.

In general, actual operations rarely occur in ordinary terrain or under ordinary conditions, but they occur in terrain that has mountains, rivers, forests, cities, or villages and in both daytime and nighttime, rain and snow, and hot and cold temperatures.

Hence, actual operations are measures best suited to the particular conditions, formulated on the basis of the estimate of the situation, coping with actual situations that include various conditions in varied aspects, with general principles of war modified or supplemented by principles under special conditions, depending upon the degree of mountainous terrain, rivers, etc.

In other words, it is necessary to aim at closely combining the principles of war of preceding Parts and this Part and at their complete application within their interacting relationships.

Chapter II.   Operations (Combat) Based upon
the Special Nature of the Terrain

1.   Effect of the special nature of the terrain upon military actions

It goes without saying that there is a close relationship between terrain and military actions.   Hence, the special nature of the terrain controls the nature of operations (engagements) that occur in that terrain.

The basic elements by which this special nature of the terrain affects military actions can be grouped in the following three categories:

    a.   Obstructions to movement

    b.   Obstructions to the field of view and field of fire

c. Obstructions to the effectiveness of firepower

In other words, by studying which of the above **three** are most notable on the basis of the special nature of the terrain and by further studying this situation, the correct nature of operations (combat) in special terrain can be understood.

2. Mountain operations

a. Characteristics of mountainous terrain

The topographic characteristics of mountainous terrain are topographic accidentedness, inclination of slope, nature of the ground, altitude, and weather, and it is rather extensive (width and depth).

The effect these exert on military operations may be summarized as follows:

(1) The operations of a unit are limited to routes of communication. Cross-country movement is not impossible but requires considerable time. However, concealment of plans is easy.

(2) Unit deployment is restricted but is easy in depth.

(3) Inter-unit coordinated action and cooperation are difficult.

(4) There is some degree of field of view and field of fire from commanding positions, but there are many dead spaces. Low terrain has absolutely no field of view or field of fire.

(5) Use of firepower has little effectiveness except for high-angle weapons.

(6) Since unit operations are restricted, concentration of fire on routes of communication, concentration areas, etc., is extremely effective.

In other words, the effect from these on military operations includes all three elements listed above, but the effect of "obstructions to movement" is particularly striking. For this reason, integrated application of combat power is restricted, and the speed of operations is extremely limited.

b. Characteristics of mountain operations

In mountain operations, the aim must be somehow to overcome the above-listed characteristics of mountainous terrain, particularly the obstructions to movement.

However, it must be noted that "mountainous terrain is not an absolute obstruction" and, on the other hand, "mountains swallow troops" and, from the above, it can be said that, in order to destroy the enemy overwhelmingly, "rather than press against mountainous terrain, press against the ocean."

Also, the characteristics of mountain operations may be described as follows:

(1) The value of routes of communication is extremely large. Hence, the focus in mountain warfare is on the struggle for routes of communication (including preventing [their] use by the enemy).

(2) Inter-unit coordination and cooperation are difficult, and independent engagements easily develop on each route of communication.

(3) Surprise attack by ground movement requires considerable time but is very effective.

(4) The situation is easily affected by the time of year and the weather, forests usually are present, and it is important to give consideration also to these.

    c.   Cautionary items in connection with offensive and defensive operations in mountainous terrain

    (1)  Attack

(a) Key terrain that secures routes of communication, particularly that controlling the line of communications, is selected as objective.

(b) A detailed and centrally controlled plan is prepared, but in implementation, authority is divided among the independent battle groups.

(c) Emphasis is placed on envelopment, the turning movement, and the surprise attack.

    (2)  Defense

(a) Use of obstructions extending in depth in mountainous terrain and securing of high ground and saddles that control routes of communication.

(b) Defeating in detail through independent engagements in each area.

(c) Devising countermeasures against envelopment, turning movements, infiltration, and airborne and heliborne attack by the enemy.

(3) In both attack and defense, along with adapting organization and equipment to the terrain, particular attention is given to ensuring logistic support.

3.  Tactical river operations

    a.   Characteristics of rivers

Rivers are "obstructions to movement."

<u>Note</u>: The degree of obstruction differs depending upon the quality of equipment,

the width, depth, and speed of the stream, nature of the riverbed soil, topography of both river banks, traffic, and weather, etc. In recent years, the degree of obstruction by rivers has been decreasing greatly for units with excellent river-crossing equipment. The discussion below is for cases in which there is a deficiency in river-crossing equipment.

The characteristic of rivers is that, in comparison with mountainous obstructions that extend in depth (long defile), the river is only a single-line (short defile) obstacle.

In other words, the front is relatively strong, but depth is deficient and lacks flexibility.

     b.   Phase in which river obstructions impede military operations

     c.   Characteristics of tactical river operations.

On the basis of the characteristics of river obstructions and the phase in which river obstructions impede military operations, the weaknesses of the attacker and defender may be listed as follows:

       (1)  Attacker

          (a)  In the initial period, posture is confused, and use of combat power is limited.

          (b)  Tactical movement and support are limited.

          (c)  Troops and equipment are divided between the two river banks.

          (d)  Special equipment and supplies are required for the river-crossing.

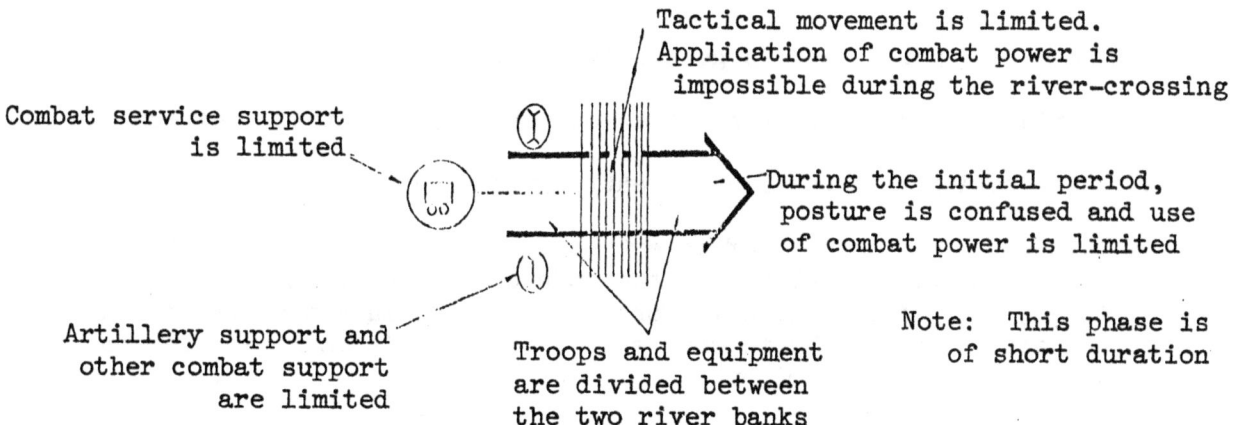

Combat service support is limited

Tactical movement is limited. Application of combat power is impossible during the river-crossing

During the initial period, posture is confused and use of combat power is limited

Artillery support and other combat support are limited

Troops and equipment are divided between the two river banks

Note: This phase is of short duration

Figure 99

(2) Defender

    (a) There is little opportunity to take advantage of weaknesses in the attack.

    (b) There is a lack of flexibility in depth and laterally.

Hence, in a river engagement, there is a race to concentrate combat power at the river-crossing point. Also, it is necessary for both offense and defense to take advantage of weaknesses of the respective opponent, and "seizure of tactical opportunities and the surprise attack" are particularly important.

  d. Cautionary items in connection with the river offensive and defensive

    (1) Attack

        (a) River-crossing as distant as possible from the enemy. (Crossing the obstruction far from the enemy.)

        (b) Keeping plans secret, for a surprise attack.

        (c) Making preparations carefully, for a one-time effort.

    (2) Defense

        (a) Attempting to make direct use of the river as an obstruction.

        (b) Taking advantage of the situation when the attacker has half his force across the river.

        (c) Striving to retain flexibility.

Note:

  1. Traversing minefields is generally similar to river-crossings.

  2. In river engagements, a position of readiness (central position) is used.

As to the position of readiness (central position):

In cases of assignment of an extremely broad front relative to one's force, in the initial phase, the zone of action of the main force is not fixed, but, first, the main force is disposed in a posture of readiness, and after determining to some extent the enemy's course of action, a decisive battle is sought.

4. Defile engagement

  a. Characteristics of the defile

Defiles are "obstructions to movement."

The defile-type obstruction is characterized by limiting evolution and deployment toward the flanks.  Hence, movement in depth is confined within narrow limits.

    b.   Unit condition produced by passing through the defile

    c.   Characteristics of the defile engagement

Outlet of defile (Farther end) — The single column, because of opening out toward the flanks, is limited in its use of combat power and requires considerable time.

Interior of defile — Because the terrain is narrow, the unit is disposed in depth, and use of combat power at the front is curtailed.

Entry of defile (Nearer end) — The unit, opened out laterally, is brought together into a single column.  Hence, the unit is jammed together and disordered.

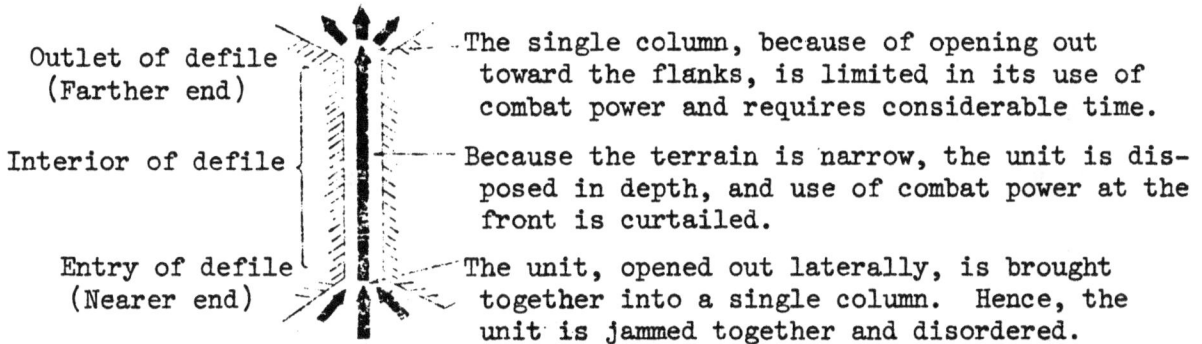

Note:  The condition of the unit differs with the size of the unit

Figure 100

On the basis of the characteristics of defiles and the conditions of defile engagements, the characteristics of the defile engagement may be listed as follows:

    (1)  The defile engagement is **very advantage**ous for the defender and extremely disadvantageous for the attacker.  (However, this disadvantage is alleviated by tactical air movement.)

    (2)  For passage through a defile, covering measures are absolutely necessary.

    (3)  In passage through a defile, it is necessary to use as many passages as possible and to pass through rapidly.

    (4)  The defile engagement differs in accordance with the situation, respectively, at the defile entrance, within the defile, and at the defile outlet.

    d.   Cautionary items in defile engagements

    (1)  Engagement near the defile entrance

The defender holds key positions near the entrance and obstructs the preparation and implementation of the passage through the defile by the attacker.

The attacker attempts to seize those key positions quickly, facilitating avoidance of disorder and the preparation and implementation of the passage.

In other words, in engagements near the entrance of the defile, key positions ("gateposts") near the entry are the focus of the attacker and the defender.

(2)  Engagements within the defile

The defender, utilizing the attacker's weakness of being limited in lateral deployment and movement, obstructs (defense or delaying action) in depth the advance of the attacker.

The attacker prepares to be able to use sufficient combat power in depth near the entry and strives to pass through in a single effort.

In other words, in the engagement within the defile, the focus is on the attacker's power to break through and charge forward.

(3)  Engagement near the defile outlet

The defender, taking advantage of the fact that the attacker advancing out of the defile has not completed the concentration of his combat power, attempts to defeat in detail (by firepower or counterattack).  At that time, by delaying the attacker in the in-depth situation as much as possible, [the defender] obstructs the attacker's concentration of combat power.

The attacker occupies key positions near the outlet and takes other measures to cover the concentration of fighting strength, prevents defeat in detail, and seeks to concentrate combat power as quickly as possible.

In other words, in engagements near the defile outlet, the focus is on active and bold action by the defender and on seizing tactical opportunities.

Note:  Multiple defile

This is a situation created by several defiles and is frequent in mountainous regions.  Multiple-defile engagements apply mountain operations.

5.  Engagements in forests and populated places

a.  Characteristics of forests and populated places

Forests and populated places, on the basis of their topographic characteristics, all include three essential elements (obstruction to movement, obstruction to field of view and field of fire, and obstruction to effectiveness of firepower), "obstruction to field of view and field of fire" being particularly marked.

For this reason, the tactical characteristics, in general, include the following:

(1)  The effectiveness of concealment and cover is great

(2)  Obstruction to fire and movement

(3) Difficulty of command and liaison

b. Characteristics of forest and urban combat

Combat in forests and populated places, by its nature, creates difficulty of collecting intelligence information and of security and facilitates surprise attack. Also, there is a tendency for units easily to become dispersed and be thrown into disorder, and concentration and use of combat power become difficult.

Hence, combat in forests and populated places requires a large force; and yet, piecemeal commitment occurs easily, because "forests and populated places swallow troops."

From this fact, in forest and urban combat, "fighting outside" (seeking the decisive engagement outside the forest or populated place) is the essence of the operation.

c. Cautionary items concerning forest and urban combat

(1) Attack

In attacking the enemy through a forest or populated place, attacking him directly from the front is avoided as much as possible, and by envelopment, a turning movement, etc., a change is effected in the surrounding general posture, and a resolution is effected by neutralizing the enemy.

In cases where it is necessary to attack those [areas] directly and in combat directed toward their interior, it is necessary to strengthen intelligence, security, and control measures and to stress close combat and the surprise attack.

(2) Defense

In the defense, forests and populated places also are used as strong points, but it is better to use them as obstructions.

In defense directly using them or in defense within them, it is necessary, as much as possible, to harass the attacker, throw him into confusion, and engage in combat with emphasis on quick-reaction firepower and local counterattack.

6. Operations in snowy and cold areas

a. Characteristics of snowy and cold areas

(1) In our country [Japan], with its relationship between snowy and cold areas and the latitude, the degree of coldness is relatively moderate, but there are many areas where the quantity of accumulated snow is large.

(2) Their most important characteristics are deep snow, snow storms, severe cold, sudden changes of weather, long nights, etc., but, within Japan, these do not make troop movement impossible.

(3)  In general, the transportation network is greatly restricted.

(4)  The snowy and cold area is "an obstruction to movement." Also, similarly, the formation of deep mud from the season of thawing of ice and melting of snow exerts a great effect on the conduct of military operations.

b.  Effect on the application of combat power

(1)  Energy of personnel

Energy of personnel, because of the cold and snow, generally becomes sluggish.

For this reason, countermeasures such as heating, keeping warm, equipment, and training are necessary, but when these are inappropriate, it is necessary to be careful not to sustain serious damage from the weather before combat with the enemy.

(2)  Application of firepower

The movement of artillery, etc., is restricted and sluggish.  Also, reliability of the supply of ammunition, etc., is particularly important.  However, the weapons' range can be used, where the target is clear.

In regard to the performance of artillery, etc., if cold-weather materials are available, there are no special problems.

(3)  Application of tactical mobility

In terrain where the degree of obstruction is low during periods when there is no accumulated snow or cold weather, the degree of obstruction increases with the accumulation of snow.  Conversely, with rivers, mountainous districts, etc., where the degree of obstruction generally is great, the degree of obstruction is decreased by freezing and snow accumulation.

Also, units that are equipped with snow-crossing equipment and are thoroughly trained, have relatively unrestricted tactical mobility, whereas a unit lacking those qualities is greatly restricted in tactical mobility even on flat terrain.

Also, the degree of obstruction differs with heavily equipped units, lightly equipped units, etc., and for heavy-vehicle units, etc., it is necessary to clear snow from roads continuously and uninterruptedly.

(4)  Logistics

The requirement for cold-resistant rations, materials, fuel, etc., increases, and exhausting them directly weakens combat power, doing this to a greater extent than in ordinary operations.

For routes of communication, in general, great effort is required to open and maintain them, and use is restricted by the weather, etc.

Hence, securing the line of communications is extremely important but extremely fragile.

c. Characteristics of operations in snowy and cold regions

(1) The success of operations is governed by the quality of preparations. In particular, secure availability of special equipment and cold-resistant materials and thorough training are extremely important.

(2) Securing the line of communications is absolutely decisive for this operation.

Chapter III. Combat Using Nighttime Darkness, etc.

1. Purpose of using nighttime darkness in combat

Nighttime darkness, that is, darkness, by its nature, permits the surprise attack, and it limits the application of combat power by both sides. Hence, the purpose of using nighttime darkness in combat is to make relative combat power advantageous by a surprise attack and reducing losses.

By developments in science and technology, it has become possible to change nighttime darkness into daytime, and there is a tendency to make daytime use of nighttime, but it still is difficult to change the entire battlefield for the entire time period into daytime, and combat using nighttime darkness still has its former importance.

Note: Difference between nighttime darkness and dense fog, etc.

With nighttime darkness, illumination is possible, and it clearly has a limit timewise, but with fog, etc., illumination is impossible, and there is great uncertainty in a situation that cannot be delimited in time or space.

In combat, depending upon the [operation's] stage in which the night darkness is utilized, there is a division into evening-dusk attack, predawn attack, dawn attack, night attack, etc.

2. Evening-dusk attack

The evening-dusk attack is an "assault ([use of] force)" applying integrated combat power of artillery, tanks, etc., and, in many cases, is an attack in a limited area.

In other words, close-combat units, applying ample firepower from the first, approach under cover of a curtain of darkness in the latter part of the period and with reduced losses from enemy firepower, and they have the advantage of being able to penetrate, the attack ending with nightfall.

In the evening-dusk attack, it is necessary to be careful to attack with the sun at one's back.

3. Predawn attack

The predawn attack, at first, is a night attack (strategem) and, thereafter, shifts to a daytime attack (force).

This attack aims at effecting a "surprise attack" (strategem) and "using daytime for the longest possible time."  It has the advantages of approach by using night and twilight to avoid observed fire from superior artillery firepower and infantry heavy weapons, gradual deployment as light increases, and being able to attack while avoiding losses, but in combat after dawn, attention must be given to enemy artillery that has not been neutralized.

4.  Dawn attack

This type of attack uses night darkness for attack preparation, and the combat phase of the attack attempts to crush the enemy with force after the dawn.

In this attack the aim is to conceal the attack preparations by means of night-time darkness and to use daytime to the maximum length.

In the dawn attack, insofar as possible, a direction of attack that faces the sun must be avoided.

5.  Night attack

   a.  The aim of the night attack is, by secret movement using the special character of nighttime darkness, to make a "surprise attack."

Hence, planning and implementation must be directed toward a surprise attack.

In other words, the plan naturally must be kept secret and is thought out on the premise that the attack time, direction, and plan of execution all permit the surprise attack (strategem).

   b.  The night attack involves some disadvantages, and an effort is made to minimize these.  Training and equipment can compensate considerably for these disadvantages, but the following, inter alia, are important for the implementation:

   Thoroughness of preparations

   Clearness of the plan

   Measures for required control

   c.  It must be realized that the tactical gains from a night attack general-ly are limited.  Generally, it is a limited attack of shallow depth.

Examples:

   Night attack by the [Japanese] 2d Division at Gong-zhang-ling [Kung-chang-ling][in the Battle of Liaoyang, 23 August-5 September 1904]

   Night attack by the [Japanese] 2d Division on Guadalcanal [Oct 1942?]

# Postscript

"Skill in application resides solely in the individual."

This book attempted to explain the most important principles of war, but merely because of having read about the principles of war, one cannot, the next day, be immediately proficient in military strategy. Simply studying the theory and academic subject alone definitely is not effective, and only by assimilating it does it have value.

Just as it is said that "all theories are gray," the principles of war also are not very clear-cut. There are not a few inconsistencies among the principles of war. (For example, mutual inconsistencies such as the principles of concentration and security in the nine principles of combat.)

The great Moltke stated as follows: "Warfare, like other arts, cannot be learned by reasoning methods. It can be learned only by the process of experience."

You will increasingly be pursuing diligent self-help study hereafter, and, with the results of study of this book as a base, you must be diligent in the study of military history, increase your understanding of the principles of war, experience an infinite variety of difficult situations, and improve your judgment in order to be able to accomplish your mission.

SELECTED BIBLIOGRAPHY

## General Works on Military Strategy

Clausewitz, Karl von. On War. Edited by Michael Howard and Peter Paret.
    Princeton, NJ: Princeton University Press, 1976.

Earle, Edward Meade, ed. Military Thought from Machiavelli to Hitler.
    Princeton, NJ: Princeton University Press, 1943.

Sun-Tzu. The Art of War. Translated and with an introduction by Samuel B.
    Griffith. New York: Oxford University Press, 1971.


## PreModern Warfare

Engels, Donald W. Alexander the Great and the Logistics of the Macedonian
    Army. Berkeley: University of California Press, 1978.

Fuller, J. F. C. The Generalship of Alexander the Great. London: Eyre and
    Spottiswode, 1958.

Storry, Richard. The Way of the Samurai. London: Orbis, 1978.

Thucydides. The History of the Peloponnesian War. Edited by Richard
    Livingstone. New York: Oxford University Press, 1960.

Turnbull, Stephen R. The Samurai: A Military History. New York:
    Macmillan, 1977.

_____. The Book of the Samurai: The Warrior Class of Japan. New York:
    Arco Publishing Co., 1982.


## 19th Century Warfare

Chandler, David G. The Campaigns of Napoleon. New York: Macmillan, 1966.

Craig, Gordon Alexander. The Battle of Koniggratz. 1964. Reprint.
    Westport, CT: Greenwood Press, 1976.

Howard, Michael. The Franco-Prussian War: The German Invasion of France,
    1870-1871. New York: Macmillan, 1961.

Moltke, Helmuth Karl Bernhard, graf von. Strategy, Its Theory and
    Application: The Wars for German Unification, 1866-1871. 1907.
    Reprint. Westport, CT: Greenwood Press, 1971.

Wagner, Arthur L. The Campaign of Koniggratz: A Study of the Austro-
    Prussian Conflict in Light of the American Civil War. 1889. Reprint.
    Westport, CT: Greenwood Press, 1972.

## Russo-Japanese War, 1904-1905

Warner, Denis A., and Peggy Warner. The Tide at Sunrise: A History of the Russo-Japanese War. New York: Charterhouse, 1974.

## World War I, 1914-1918 -- Western Front

Barnett, Correlli. The Swordbearers: Supreme Command in the First World War. Bloomington: Indiana University Press, 1975.

Falls, Cyril H. The Battle of Caporetto. Philadelphia: Lippincott, 1966.

Horne, Alistair. The Price of Glory: Verdun, 1916. New York: Penguin Books, 1979.

Liddell Hart, Basil Henry. The Real War, 1914-1918. Boston: Little, Brown, 1963.

Moorehead, Alan. Gallipoli. New York: Harper, 1956.

Rommel, Erwin. Attacks. 1937. Reprint. Vienna, VA: Athena Press, 1979.

Wolff, Leon. In Flanders Fields: The 1917 Campaign. New York: Viking, 1958.

## World War I -- Eastern Front

Golovin, Nikolai N. The Russian Army in World War I. 1931. Reprint. Hamden, CT: Shoe String Press, 1969.

Stone, Norman. The Eastern Front, 1914-1917. New York: Scribner, 1975.

## World War II, 1939-1945

### Western Europe

Cole, Hugh M. The Ardennes: Battle of the Bulge. The United States Army in World War II: The European Theater of Operations. Washington, DC: Office of the Chief of Military History, Department of the Army, 1965.

Guderian, Heinz. Panzer Leader. Translated from the German by Constantine Fitzgibbon. New York: Dutton, 1952.

Harrison, Gordon A. Cross Channel Attack. The United States Army in World War II: The European Theater of Operations. Washington, DC: Office of the Chief of Military History, Department of the Army, 1951.

Horne, Alistair. _To Lose a Battle: France, 1940_. Boston: Little, Brown, 1969.

Matloff, Maurice, and Edwin M. Snell. _Strategic Planning for Coalition Warfare, 1941-1942--1943-1944_. 2 vols. The United States Army in World War II: The War Department. Washington, DC: Office of the Chief of Military History, Department of the Army, 1953-1959.

Mellenthin, Friedrich Wilhelm von. _Panzer Battles: A Study of the Employment of Armor in the Second World War_. Translated by H. Betzler; edited by L. C. F. Turner. Norman: University of Oklahoma Press, 1956.

Young, Desmond. _Rommel, The Desert Fox_. New York: Harper, 1950.


## Eastern Front

Carell, Paul. _Hitler Moves East, 1941-1943_. Boston: Little, Brown, 1965.

Clark, Alan. _Barbarossa: The Russian-German Conflict, 1941-45_. New York: Morrow, 1965.

Erickson, John. _The Road to Stalingrad_. New York: Harper & Row, 1975.

Ziemke, Earl F. _Stalingrad to Berlin: The German Defeat in the East_. Army Historical Series. Washington, DC: Office of the Chief of Military History, U.S. Army, 1968.


## Pacific

Appleman, Roy E. _Okinawa: The Last Battle_. The United States Army in World War II: The War in the Pacific. Washington, DC: Historical Division, Department of the Army, 1948.

Baker, P. _Atomic Bomb: The Great Decision_. 2d ed. New York: Holt, Rinehart and Winston, 1976.

Campbell, Arthur F. _The Siege: A Story from Kohima_. New York: Macmillan, 1956.

Crowl, Philip A. _Campaign in the Marianas_. The United States Army in World War II: The War in the Pacific. Washington, DC: Office of the Chief of Military History, Department of the Army, 1960.

Evans, Geoffrey C., Sir, and Antony Brett-James. _Imphal, A Flower on Lofty Heights_. New York: St. Martin's Press, 1962.

Falk, Stanley L. _Seventy Days to Singapore_. New York: Putnam, 1975.

Feis, Herbert. _The Atomic Bomb and the End of World War II_. Rev. ed. Princeton, NJ: Princeton University Press, 1966.

Griffith, Samuel B. _The Battle for Guadalcanal_. New York: Lippincott, 1963.

Hayashi, S., and Alvin D. Coox. _Kogun: The Japanese Army in the Pacific War_. Quantico, VA: Marine Corps Association, 1959.

Hough, Frank O. _The Island War: The United States Marine Corps in the Pacific_. Philadelphia: Lippincott, 1947.

Milner, Samuel. _Victory in Papua_. The United States Army in World War II: The War in the Pacific. Washington, DC: Office of the Chief of Military History, Department of the Army, 1959.

Morton, Louis. _The Fall of the Philippines_. The United States Army in World War II: The War in the Pacific. Washington, DC: Office of the Chief of Military History, Department of the Army, 1953.

Slim, William Slim, 1st viscount. _Defeat into Victory_. London: Cassell, 1956.

Smith, Robert R. _The Approach to the Philippines_. The United States Army in World War II: The War in the Pacific. Washington, DC: Office of the Chief of Military History, Department of the Army, 1953.

Toland, John. _The Rising Sun: The Decline and Fall of the Japanese Empire, 1936-1945_. New York: Random House, 1970.

Tsuji, Masanobu. _Singapore: The Japanese Version_. Translated by Margaret E. Lake; edited by H. V. Howe. New York: St. Martin's Press, 1960.


Korean War, 1950-1953

Appleman, Roy E. _South to the Naktong, North to the Yalu, June-November 1950_. United States Army in the Korean War. Washington, DC: Office of the Chief of Military History, Department of the Army, 1961.

Fehrenbach, T. R. _This Kind of War: A Study in Unpreparedness_. New York: Macmillan, 1963.

Heinl, Robert D. _Victory at High Tide: The Inchon-Seoul Campaign_. Philadephia, 1968.

Leckie, Robert. _Conflict: The History of the Korean War, 1950-53_. New York: Putnam, 1962.

Ridgway, Matthew B. _The Korean War_. Garden City, NY: Doubleday Books, 1967.

## Arab-Israeli Wars

Adan, Avraham (Bren). On the Banks of the Suez: An Israeli General's Personal Account of the Yom Kippur War. San Francisco: Presidio Press, 1980. (Covers the 1973 War.)

Herzog, Chaim. The Arab-Israeli Wars: War and Peace in the Middle East. New York: Random House, 1982.

London Sunday Times Insight Team. The Yom Kippur War. New York: Doubleday and Co., 1978.

Marshall, S. L. A. Swift Sword: The Historical Record of Israel's Victory, June, 1967. New York: American Heritage Publishing Co., 1967.

O'Ballance, Edgar. No Victor, No Vanquished. San Rafael, CA: Presidio Press, 1979.

Palit, D. K. Return to Sinai: The Arab Offensive, October 1973. Dehra Dun, India: Palit and Palit Publishers, 1974.

Shazly, Saad el. The Crossing of the Suez. San Francisco: American Mideast Research, 1980.

## Indochina and Vietnam

### Indochina War, 1946-1953

Fall, Bernard B. Hell in a Very Small Place: The Siege of Dien Bien Phu. Philadelphia: Lippincott, 1967.

____. Street Without Joy. 4th ed. Harrisburg, PA: Stackpole Books, 1964.

Roy, Jules. The Battle of Dienbienphu. New York: Harper & Row, 1965.

### Vietnam Conflict, 1961-1975

Elliott-Bateman, Michael. Defeat in the East: The Mark of Mao Tse-Tung on War. New York: Oxford University Press, 1967.

Herring, George C. America's Longest War: The United States and Vietnam, 1950-1975. New York: Wiley, 1979.

Lewy, Guenter. America in Vietnam. New York: Oxford University Press, 1978.

Palmer, Dave Richard. Summons of the Trumpet: U.S.-Vietnam in Perspective. San Rafael, CA: Presidio Press, 1978.

Summers, Harry G. On Strategy: The Vietnam War in Context. Carlisle Barracks, PA: Strategic Studies Institute, U.S. Army War College, 1981.